# The HOME INVADERS

# Donald E. Wildmon

Executive Director,
National Federation for Decency

VICTOR
**BOOKS** a division of SP Publications, Inc.
WHEATON. ILLINOIS 60187

*Offices also in*
Whitby, Ontario, Canada
Amersham-on-the-Hill, Bucks, England

*Fourth printing, 1986*

All Scripture quotations are from the *King James Version.*

Recommended Dewey Decimal Classification: 175.1
Suggested Subject Heading: CHRISTIANITY AND THE MEDIA

Library of Congress Catalog Card Number: 84-52366
ISBN: 0-89693-521-3

# CONTENTS

# INTRODUCTION

The organized church in America faces the greatest threat to its existence since our country was founded. I fully realize how extreme that statement sounds.

There is an intentional effort among many of the leaders of our media to reshape our society, to replace the Christian view of man as our foundation with the humanist view of man. That is what this book is about. While *The Home Invaders* deals primarily with television, the problem is by no means confined to that medium. Why the emphasis on television? Because it is the most powerful educator in our society.

The networks refuse to sell airtime to any Christian organization. Does that mean that there are no religious programs on the networks? Nothing could be further from the truth. Most of the network programs carry a religious message, but one that is rooted in humanism.

That I would be writing a book like this surprises no one any more than it does me. While I have done a fair amount of writing in the past (eighteen books), it was all in the devotional/inspirational area. The positions taken in this book were arrived at not by whim, but because I had no other choice than to be intellectually honest.

DONALD E. WILDMON

# ONE

# DEFINING THE PROBLEM

One night during the Christmas holidays of 1976, I decided to watch television with my family. Gathered around the set in our den, shortly after 7 P.M., we prepared ourselves for a relaxing time of entertainment. We turned on the set and sat back to be entertained.

Not far into the program was a scene of adultery. I reacted to the situation in the manner I had been taught. I asked one of the children to change channels. Getting involved in the second program, we were shocked with some crude profanity. Once again reacting in the prescribed manner, I asked one of the children to change the channel. We got involved in a mystery when, without warning, on came a totally unexpected scene in which one man had another tied down and was working him over with a hammer. I again reacted as I had been instructed. I asked one of the children to turn off the set.

As I sat in my den that night, I became angry. I had been disturbed by the deterioration of morals I had witnessed in the media and society during the previous twenty-five years. This was accompanied by a dramatic rise in crime, a proliferation of pornography, increasingly explicit sexual lyrics in music, increasing numbers of broken homes, a rise in drug and alcohol use among the youth, and various other negative factors. I had managed to avoid those unpleasant changes to a large degree by staying away, turning my head, justifying my actions with the reasons most commonly expressed—freedom of speech, pluralism, tolerance.

Realizing that these changes were being brought into the sanctity of my home, I decided I could and would no longer remain silent. I decided to do something, even though at the time I had no idea what that something would be. Little did I realize the magnitude of my decision.

Out of that decision came the National Federation for Decency (and out of the NFD came the Coalition for Better Television). For nearly three years I dealt with what I perceived to be the problems with television—sex, violence, and profanity. But the more I dealt with the problems, the more I realized that I was dealing only with symptoms—not the disease.

I began to notice the manner in which Christians were presented in network programs—when indeed, they were presented. I began to look at the values television was teaching. I came to the conclusion that Christians were discriminated against. For months I studied the situation, all the while refusing to address it publicly.

## I Decided That I Must Speak Out

Finally, I decided that I must speak out on this issue. On September 24, 1981 I gave a speech to the National Broadcasters Association for Community Affairs in Vail, Colorado. I addressed the problem of religious discrimination by the networks in their programs. The audience was the most hostile I have ever encountered. Reactions during the speech included not only hisses and rejections, but vicious profanity hurled toward me because of what I was saying. I even left out a significant portion of the speech in order to finish more quickly. I could not understand the reaction at the time, but as the months passed I understood.

For the next several months I spoke out against this anti-Christian discrimination. The more I spoke out, the more those in the industry reacted viciously. Network officials compared me with Hitler, McCarthy, and the Ayatollah Khomeini. James Rosenfield, president of CBS, referred to me as the "ayatollah of the religious right."

Why this viciousness toward me when I was doing nothing more than suggesting selective buying and selective viewing? Other groups, including homosexuals, had done the same thing for years and yet the networks and other media had never reacted in such a vicious manner. It was a mystery to me until I learned that what those who opposed me really resented was the fact that I was a Christian and was motivated by my Christian faith. That was the problem. Gene Mater, a vice-president of CBS, told me in a debate in Los Angeles: "What sets you apart . . . is the fact that you are . . . cloaked in this self-assumed aura of religious respectability."

Now let me tarry no longer with the history of my cause at this point. Most people are somewhat familiar with it. I must go deeper and state the real issue. It is far greater than sex and violence on television. At stake is the very foundation on which Western civilization is built.

Because of my work, I have crossed paths with many leaders in the "moral revolution" during the past few years. One term which kept popping up from many of these leaders was "secular humanism." I avoided that term like the plague; people who used it made me feel very uncomfortable. These people were trying to make things too simple, too pat. They were trying to make visible an invisible force.

Nonetheless, there was something about network television which continued to worry me, something which I could not put my finger on. I kept looking, searching, trying to find the root of the disturbance. I finally found the answer. Before I tell you that answer, I want to share some other information with you.

Shortly after I got involved in this work, someone gave me a copy of a book entitled *Television: Ethics for Hire?* I did not think I had time to read it so I laid it aside. Several months later I took the book down from the shelf and discovered that it was written by Dr. Robert S. Alley (and published by Abingdon Press, the publishing division of the United Methodist Church). I had met Dr. Alley, who at that time was professor of religion and chairman of the department at the University of Richmond, on a television talk show in Oklahoma City. He was extremely hostile, but this was not unusual and I really thought little about it. Now I decided to see what this man had to say in his book. Much time and research had gone into its preparation, and I found Dr. Alley's observations quite interesting.

"One of the presumed values of our culture which is deeply embedded in most all traditions is the authority of the home. (An underlying assumption of this book is that such authority has eroded dramatically in the past two decades and that television has played a major role in that erosion)," wrote Dr. Alley. So far, so good. I completely agreed.

## Humanists Urged to Use the Media
But as I continued to read, I realized that Dr. Alley is in reality an advocate of humanism. Consider this statement in his book: "The printing press undoubtedly caused a decline in the production of illuminated pages in manuscripts, thereby conceivably resulting in the loss of a distinct art form, but that same press helped create a cultural and intellectual revolution whose influences still excite his-

torians. *Likewise, in the twentieth century it would appear that humanists might bear heavy responsibility for alerting citizens to alternative patterns of living and learning made mandatory by scientific advance comparable to the Gutenberg era"* (italics mine). I found this reference to humanists using television to educate and inform interesting, all the more so since no reference was made that Christians could or should do the same.

In referring to Jim Brooks, producer of the "Mary Tyler Moore Show," Dr. Alley wrote: "He (Brooks) is reticent to allow Mary to presume to 'comment on issues'; yet she and the cast *do take positions on women's rights, sex, impotence, homosexuality, smoking, planned parenthood, marriage, divorce, religion, the communications industry, and medicine.* All these have received significant comment in the last six years. So even though it is 'not our object to say anything,' according to the producer (Brooks), *MTM speaks effectively to the society of the seventies"* (italics mine).

Continuing to discuss the "Mary Tyler Moore Show," Dr. Alley wrote: "Most viewers would see Mary as a product of American Protestant ethics, interpreted through the culture, *albeit conditioned by enlightened humanism.* Mary is free of dogma and is not judgmental. Her ethics are personal, individual" (italics mine). The gist of the statement is that had Mary maintained her Protestant ethics minus the "enlightened humanism," she would not have been such an acceptable person.

Later, commenting on the program "M\*A\*S\*H," Dr. Alley wrote: "Larry Gelbart, producer of 'M\*A\*S\*H,' leaves the impression of concurring with (Alan) Alda that 'M\*A\*S\*H' 'presents a very strong humanist point of view.' Of TV drama and comedy Alda noted that the *'message gets across in inverse proportion to its being made conscious,'* for *'the unspoken assumptions are what mold the audience'* " (italics mine).

Continuing his observation concerning "M\*A\*S\*H," Dr. Alley wrote: "The religious perspective of the series is humanism." He later adds, *"This exceptionally well-conceived alternative to traditional dogma, cast in terms of secular humanism, might be an appropriate focus for religious institutions to reexamine their exclusivistic assumptions . . . "* (italics mine)

Now what makes this matter of more than passing importance is that "M\*A\*S\*H" was the closest thing to a modern-day setting for a continuing series which featured a Christian. Yet the Christian on "M\*A\*S\*H" (the chaplain) was, at best, depicted as an incompetent, awkward, and irrelevant fixture.

A few years ago I came across a quote by Dr. Rose K. Goldsen, professor of sociology at Cornell University, which caught my attention. "TV is more than just a little fun and entertainment. It's a whole environment, and what it does bears an unpleasant resemblance to behavior modification on a mass scale." I watched television more closely with Dr. Goldsen's comment in mind. Clearly the networks are intentionally pushing a particular value system. That value system is humanism. That was what had been disturbing me.

## Tenets of Humanism

What are the basic tenets of humanism? Let me quote them directly from the documents *Humanist Manifesto I* and *II,* the "bible" of the humanist:

1. Religious humanists regard the universe as self-existing and not created.

2. Humanism believes that man is a part of nature and that he has emerged as the result of a continuous process.

3. Humanism asserts that the nature of the universe depicted by modern science makes unacceptable any supernatural or cosmic guarantees of human values.

4. Humanists are firmly convinced that existing acquisitive and profit-motivated society has shown itself to be inadequate and that a radical change in methods, controls, and motives must be instituted.

5. We find insufficient evidence for belief in the existence of a supernatural; it is either meaningless or irrelevant to the question of the survival and fulfillment of the human race . . . no deity will save us; we must save ourselves.

6. Promises of immortal salvation or fear of eternal damnation are both illusory and harmful.

7. Ethics is autonomous and situational, needing no theological or ideological sanction.

8. Reason and intelligence are the most effective instruments that humankind possesses. There is no substitute; neither faith nor passion. . . .

9. In the area of sexuality, we believe that intolerant attitudes, often cultivated by orthodox religions and puritanical cultures, unduly repress sexual conduct. While we do not approve of exploitive, denigrating forms of

sexual expression, neither do we wish to prohibit, by law or social sanction, sexual behavior between consenting adults. The right to . . . abortion . . . should be recognized.

10. To enhance freedom and dignity, the individual must experience a full range of civil liberties in all societies. This includes . . . a recognition of an individual's right to die with dignity, euthanasia, and the right to suicide.

11. We look to the development of a system of world law and a world order based on transnational federal government.

12. Humanists . . . believe that traditional theism, especially faith in the prayer-hearing God, assumed to love and care for persons, to hear and understand their prayers, and to be able to do something about them, is an unproved and outmoded faith. Salvationism, based on mere affirmation, still appears as harmful, diverting people with false hopes of heaven hereafter. Reasonable minds must look to other means for survival.

Simply stated, humanism is a religion which teaches that man is his own god. Humanism places man at the center and makes him the measure of all things.

In writing about the "moral revolution" in his book *What Is Secular Humanism?* the noted historian and professor of history at St. Louis University, Dr. James Hitchcock, says: "Television has been by far its [secular humanism's] chief disseminator. It would be almost impossible to overestimate its influence. Just as destructive as its concentration on what is deviant and amoral has been television's general ignoring of religion as a positive force. . . . When providing viewers with fictional images of what life is like, television rarely adverts to the fact that, for a great majority of Americans, religious belief is an integral part of their lives. Religiously motivated characters [on TV] are likely to be neurotics for whom religion is a form of sickness. Rarely are sympathetic characters presented whose lives are strengthened by prayer or the guidance of clergy. Millions of Americans attend church on Sunday and pray in their homes, but rarely are they shown doing this on television."

For some time now, I have been saying (and getting severely criticized for doing so), that network television is anti-Christian and is being used to reshape the values which undergird our society. It was interesting to read a statement made by Dr. Claire Randall, general secretary of the National Council of Churches: "There seems to be a pattern in '60 Minutes' programming of doing negative and critical pieces about organized religion—Protestants, Catholics, evangelicals—which results in creating mistrust and doubt." Bishop Emerson S. Colaw, referring to television, wrote in the *United Methodist Reporter*: "There does seem to be some kind of persistent effort to cheapen the sacred and demean the traditional institutions that form the glue of our society. Perhaps we should not be so passive in our acceptance." It is refreshing to note that other Christians, coming from different perspectives, are beginning to see this anti-Christian orientation of the networks.

## Media "Blesses" Hollywood Social Reformers

While the media has consistently condemned television ministers in the past few years, there has been practically no condemnation of the Hollywood leaders of social reform. The individual who has used television more than any other to preach his doctrine is not a household evangelical name. It is Norman Lear. The difference between Lear's preaching and other television ministers is only in style and substance.

Lear founded People for the American Way and has mailed hundreds of thousands of letters asking for money to support his ministry. One of his largest supporters is the Playboy Foundation, the anti-Christian group which exploits women for profit and promotes the use of illegal drugs and the pursuit of hedonism.

The people responsible for network television are "preaching" just as much as any preacher in any pulpit. They are using television to preach their humanist religion to the impressionable children of America. Jesus said: "Suffer the little children to come unto Me, and forbid them not" (Mark 10:14). But these people obviously do not want little children to come under the influence of Christ.

Traditional Christian values take a real beating on network television. Early in my current ministry I would have been uncomfortable making such a statement. I realize that many people still are uncomfortable with it. However, I must speak the truth as God leads me to see the truth, even if it is uncomfortable.

During the past few years the number of programs on network television directly mocking Christianity, Christian values, and Christian morals has increased at a rapid pace. This conclusion is confirmed each day as I look at the reports sent in by hundreds of monitors involved in the Coalition for Better Television's monitoring program, and as these programs are reviewed in our office. The general public usually looks at the programming in bits and pieces. Mine is an overview.

Pollster George Gallup stated that 90 percent of the people in this country identify with the Christian faith. *The censorship against Christians by network television is so complete that not one continuing series set in a modern-day setting has a single person who is identified as a Christian!* In fact, when Christians are depicted in programs with modern-day settings, they nearly always are stereotyped as being hypocrites, liars, cheats, frauds, unfaithful in their marriage vows, etc.

On November 13, 1982 NBC aired an episode of "Taxi" which depicted a priest (the viewer was led to believe that the priest was Greek Orthodox) recommending to a parishioner that she commit adultery with a friend of her husband. The priest said this was necessary for reconciliation because her husband had committed adultery. Here is the dialogue, taken from the program, which involves the husband (Latka), wife (Simka), and priest (Rev. Gorky).

REV. GORKY: Since Latka sinned with someone he worked with, Simka must sin with someone Latka works with. (Rev. Gorky exits.)

SIMKA: You see what we must do.

LATKA: You mean you're going to go through with this?

SIMKA: Latka, we are religious people. We are orthodox. Our church has told us what we must do. And we must obey if we are to remain married.

LATKA: You mean to tell me you're going to sleep with one of my friends? (Simka nods affirmatively.) Baby, you're the greatest! (Canned laughter.)

Dr. Miltiades B. Efthimiou of the Greek Orthodox Church, a friend of mine, wrote me concerning the program. He was upset at the growing tendency among the three major networks to portray those of the Christian faith in the worst possible light. He was shocked and alarmed at the manner in which priests of his own faith had been ridiculed by this episode of NBC's "Taxi."

### No Positive Portrayal of Christians

Name one network program, set in a modern-day setting, which has depicted a Christian as a warm, loving, intelligent, compassionate human being. After seven years of studying television, I cannot recall a single character, depicted as a Christian in a modern-day setting, who was shown in a positive manner.

Four of every five intercourse scenes on television involve people not married to each other. Adultery is never shown as being immoral. By the time a youngster has graduated from high school, he has seen more than 18,000 murders on television. Homosexuals are nearly always shown in a good light. (The National Gay Media Task Force is consulted by the networks to review all programs involving presentations of homosexuals and the networks nearly always follow the NGMTF suggestions. The NGMTF is even paid for this service.)

The greatest educator in our nation is not the school, or the church, or even the home. It is television. A youngster who graduates from high school has spent 50 percent more time in front the television than in the classroom. The values and morals of the networks are diametrically different from those of the vast majority of our homes.

Let me move from television for a moment into a related area. Dr. Alan Walker, director of the World Methodist Council's evangelism emphasis and widely known for his social activism as well as evangelism, has called for a strong crusade against pornography. "Christian forces must organize, before it is too late, to halt a deepening corruption of Western society," Dr. Walker said. Pornography is now a multi-billion dollar business. It exploits and degrades humanity. It has become so acceptable that R.J. Reynolds, the company which owns Del Monte Foods and Kentucky Fried Chicken, sinks millions of dollars into promoting it via advertisements in the pornographic magazines. In addition, the number-one seller of pornographic magazines in this country is not the adult bookstores but 7-Eleven convenience stores. Both R.J. Reynolds and 7-Eleven justify their positions on the basis that pornography is a good moneymaker for them. Divorce capitalism from Christian ethics and you have an economic system which makes Communism look like a Sunday School picnic.

Now the question, "Where has the church been during all of this?" The voice of the organized, institutional church has, for the most part, been silent, and that silence has been deafening!

The church has taken its stand in the area of civil rights, injustice, hunger, human rights, and other fields—as it should. It is called of God to do so. But the church must not, cannot, neglect the moral breakdown in our society resulting from the media's promotion of humanism, a religion which acknowledges no God and views man as only an accident; a religion which has no place for a Man hanging on a cross who, in His silence, called man to repentance and involvement; a religion which says that belief in Jesus Christ, the Son of God, is harmful to the welfare of society.

Too often the church has only echoed the voice of the humanists. We have blamed the moral deterioration in our society on economics. The humanist says that with enough money the ills of our society can be cured. The Christian cannot accept that. While the Christian fully recognizes the need for the material, the Christian also recognizes that man cannot live by bread alone, that he has a Creator and without a loving relationship with his Creator, life will always be incomplete. Therefore we are confronted with the eternal question asked by Christ Himself: "What shall it profit a man, if he gain the whole world, and lose his own soul?" (Mark 8:36) Dr. Karl Menninger wrote a book several years ago entitled *What Became of Sin?* In our attempts to deal with society from the humanist perspective, we have too often ignored man's broken relationship with God and the fact that man is a sinner needing forgiveness and reconciliation.

What good is it if we build a society where everyone has a guaranteed income of $50,000 yearly, the best health and dental care, plenty of food and housing, and the best schools possible if humans in that society perceive themselves to be nothing more than animals and proceed to act like animals? It is the duty and the responsibility of the church to act as salt, to call society back to saneness and sensibility. If we fail to do so, we will have lost our savor and deservingly will be cast out and trodden underfoot.

Let me hasten to add for those who reject what I have said, I hope and pray to God that I am totally, completely, and absolutely wrong. It would thrill me to die knowing that I was mistaken.

I feel we have two choices. Take what I have said as nonsense and go on ignoring the intentional, promoted changes in our society. Or join the effort to try to correct the situation.

As for my personal opinion, if we fail to act now, our children—probably certainly our grandchildren—will suffer for no other reason than a desire to practice their Christian faith. It can't happen, someone says. The question is not, "Can it happen?" The question is, "Will it happen?" Our system of government is a noble experiment, the first of its kind in the history of man. It is not self-perpetuating. It is not infallible. It can be destroyed.

If the church fails to rise to this challenge, then the freedom we have known in this country for more than 200 years—the envy of every nation in the world—will be over. The history of a nation which undergirded itself with Christian principles and ethics, a nation which based its law and justice on the Christian concept of man, a nation which took capitalism and nurtured it with Christian roots, a nation which has been the most giving and forgiving nation in the history of civilization, will draw to a close. The chances that any nation can ever produce such a society again are nil.

## DISCUSSION AND REFLECTION QUESTIONS

1. Do you think the author is correct when he refers to network television as anti-Christian?
2. Do you feel the promotion of humanism by the media should be a matter of major concern or that it really is not all that serious an issue?
3. Do you agree with the statement by Dr. Goldsen that TV "bears an unpleasant resemblance to behavior modification on a mass scale"?
4. At which points are the basic tenets of humanism and Christianity in agreement? At which points do they conflict?
5. Do you feel there is an intentional effort by certain segments of the media to belittle and demean the Christian faith?
6. Do you think the media has a double standard for recognized Christians who speak out on moral and social issues and liberal humanists who do the same?
7. Why do you think the media is reluctant to present a positive view of Christians and Christianity?
8. Have you seen a network television program in which homosexuality was depicted as a sin?
9. Do you agree that television is the greatest educator in our society?
10. Why hasn't the church spoken out on the moral social issues in addition to the civil social issues?
11. Do you feel the issues are as critical as the author states in the last paragraph of this chapter?

# TWO

# THE SILENCE OF THE CHURCH IS DEAFENING

In connection with the murders of five young boys in Salt Lake County, Utah, Arthur Gary Bishop was charged with five counts of first-degree murder, five counts of aggravated kidnapping, two counts of sexual abuse of a child, two counts of forcible sexual abuse, and one count of sexual exploitation of a minor.

County attorney Ted Cannon told reporters that the suspect gave authorities permission to search his house. In Bishop's home they found pornography. In fact, the police found a great deal of pornography—films, videotapes, and pictures. Among the photos were pictures of at least one of the victims after he had been kidnapped.

It is a story which could be repeated again and again. Greedy, selfish pornographers preying on the sick and perverted at the expense of innocent and defenseless children. Yet the philosophy which encourages and promotes this sickness has gone unchallenged by the church. Why?

In the last two decades, this country has been the scene of a media attack, unparalleled in history, on Christian values and the Christian faith. Our television screens feature graphic violence night after night. Not only do the networks flood us with mental and moral pornography, but in many cities hardcore pornography is shown regularly over cable or subscription television.

In order to understand this anti-Christian attack, we must understand who controls the media. Three studies by the research team of Lichter and Rothman provide insight. The first study involved hour-long interviews with 240 journalists and broadcasters at the most influential media outlets, including the *New York Times*, the *Washington Post*, the *Wall Street Journal*, *Time* magazine, *Newsweek*,

*U.S. News and World Report,* and the news departments at CBS, NBC, ABC, and PBS, along with major public broadcasting stations.

The second study involved 104 individuals called by Lichter-Rothman "the cream of television's creative community." They included fifteen presidents of independent production companies, eighteen executive producers, forty-three additional producers, twenty-six of whom are also writers, and ten network vice-presidents responsible for program development and selection. Among these, according to Lichter-Rothman, "are some of the most experienced and respected members of the craft. Many have been honored with Emmy Awards, and a few are household names. More important, this group has had a major role in shaping the shows whose themes and stars have become staples of our popular culture."

The third study featured the most successful moviemakers in Hollywood.

Here is what these scholarly studies revealed. Please keep in mind that this information does not come from those doing research for "religious" reasons, but from a research team merely reporting empirical data. The figures listed under the "News Media" column represent those of the first study involving the news elite. The figures under the "TV" column represent those of the second study involving the entertainment elite. And the figures under the "Movie" column represent the moviemakers.

| BACKGROUNDS | NEWS MEDIA | TV ELITE | MOVIE |
|---|---|---|---|
| White | 95% | 99 | 99 |
| Male | 79 | 98 | 99 |
| From Northeast or North Central states | 68 | 56 | — |
| From Northeast or West Coast | — | — | 73 |
| From metropolitan area | 42 | 82 | 81 |
| Father graduated college | 40 | 35 | — |
| Father occupation "professional" | 40 | — | — |
| College graduate | 93 | 75 | 63 |
| Postgraduate study | 55 | — | — |
| Income $30,000 | 78 | — | — |
| Family income $50,000 | 46 | — | — |
| Family income $200,000 | — | 63 | 64 |
| Political liberal | 54 | 75 | 66 |

| PRESIDENTIAL VOTING RECORDS | NEWS MEDIA | TV ELITE | MOVIE |
|---|---|---|---|
| **1964** | | | |
| Goldwater | 6% | — | — |
| Johnson | 94 | — | — |
| **1968** | | | |
| Nixon | 13 | 17 | 17 |
| Humphrey | 87 | 80 | 76 |
| **1972** | | | |
| Nixon | 19 | 15 | 18 |
| McGovern | 81 | 82 | 82 |
| **1976** | | | |
| Ford | 19 | 25 | 22 |
| Carter | 81 | 72 | 78 |
| **1980** | | | |
| Reagan | — | 20 | 29 |
| Carter | — | 49 | 51 |
| Anderson | — | 27 | 17 |

| ATTITUDE ON SOCIAL ISSUES | NEWS MEDIA | TV ELITE | MOVIE |
|---|---|---|---|
| Woman has right to decide on abortion | 90% | 97 | 96 |
| Strongly agree homosexuality is wrong | 9 | 5 | 7 |
| Strongly agree homosexuals should not teach in public schools | 3 | 6 | 4 |
| Strongly agree adultery is wrong | 15 | 16 | 13 |
| Government should redistribute income | — | 69 | 59 |
| Government should reduce income gap | 68 | — | — |
| Government should guarantee jobs | 48 | 45 | 38 |
| Structure of society causes alienation | 49 | 62 | 62 |
| Institutions need overhaul | 28 | 43 | 51 |

| RELIGIOUS ORIENTATION | NEWS MEDIA | TV ELITE | MOVIE |
|---|---|---|---|
| Jewish* | 23% | 59 | 62 |
| Protestant* | 20 | 25 | — |
| Catholic* | 12 | 12 | — |
| Religion "none" | 50 | 44 | 55 |
| Seldom or never attend worship | 86 | 93 | 96 |

*2½% of the American population is Jewish, 67% is Protestant, and 22% is Catholic.

| ATTITUDES TOWARD TV ENTERTAINMENT | NEWS MEDIA | TV ELITE | MOVIE |
|---|---|---|---|
| TV should promote social reform | — | 66% | 67 |
| Strongly agree that TV is too critical of traditional values | — | 1 | 1 |

| RANKS OF INFLUENCE | TV ELITE | MOVIE |
|---|---|---|
| *Perceived Influence* | *Preferred Influence* | *Preferred Influence* |
| 1. Media | 1. Consumer groups | 1. Intellectuals |
| 2. Business | 2. Intellectuals | 2. Consumer groups |
| 3. Government agencies | 3. Blacks | 3. Media |
| 4. Unions | 4. Feminists | 4. Blacks |
| 5. Military | 5. Business | 5. Business |
| 6. Consumer groups (7th on movie-makers' list) | 6. Media | 6. Feminists |
| 7. Religion (6th on movie- | 7. Unions | 7. Unions |

| | TV ELITE | MOVIE |
|---|---|---|
| maker's list) | | |
| 8. Intellectuals | 8. Government agencies | 8. Government agencies |
| 9. Blacks | 9. Religion | 9. Religion |
| 10. Feminists | 10. Military | 10. Military |

These studies confirm the fact that the vast majority of leaders in both the national news media and the entertainment media are overtly hostile to the Christian faith.

Notice that the TV elite and the moviemakers desire religion to have practically no influence in society. Quoting the authors on their study of the entertainment elite: *"Moreover, two out of three believe that TV entertainment should be a major force for social reform. This is perhaps the single most striking finding in our study. According to television's creators, they are not in it just for the money. They also seek to move their audience toward their own vision of the good society"* (italics mine).

Study the above information carefully. You need to be very familiar with it so you can understand what I say in this book.

Ben Stein, in *The View from Sunset Boulevard*, which followed two years of research with many leaders in Hollywood, concurred with these findings. "By definition, the people who write TV shows and produce them are not at all devout," Stein said.

When I use the term "anti-Christian" in this book, I don't mean that the elite in Hollywood and at the networks are merely apathetic toward the Christian faith; I mean they are openly hostile toward it. I use it in the same context as a black would in speaking of the Ku Klux Klan as being racist, or as a Jew would in saying that Hitler was anti-Semitic. I realize that many will think that my classification of these people as anti-Christian is perhaps a bit strong. But an example of this hostility toward Christianity is found in the rating given Billy Graham's movie, *The Prodigal*. When it came time to rate the film, Hollywood gave it a "PG," the same rating it gave *Footloose, Unfaithfully Yours,* and *Terms of Endearment*.

"PG" means that parental guidance should be used in allowing children to view a particular film. Parental guidance is usually applied to the sex, violence, or profanity a film contains. However, that was not the reason for the "PG" given Dr. Graham's film. Why, then, did Hollywood give *The Prodigal* a "PG"? One person close to those who made the decision said that the "PG" rating was given because, "Preteenage children should not be exposed to Christianity without their parents' consent."

Christian values, according to Hollywood, are dangerous and no child should be exposed to them without their parents' consent. You must remember that the Billy Graham film was not produced by Hollywood. Does Hollywood use the same label for those movies which promote the values of humanism, the religion to which most movie and network elite subscribe? No. No film which Hollywood has produced has ever been given a "PG" rating because of its religious content. Films promoting humanism, hedonism, and materialism need no warning. But films produced by Dr. Graham or other Christians are not treated in the same manner.

Of the people who are responsible for our films, 96 percent said they seldom or never attend church worship services and 55 percent claimed no religion at all. Sixty-two percent identified themselves as Jewish. When asked how much influence religion should have in our society, the elite group said practically none, ranking religion next to last on their list.

That there is a double standard used by Hollywood is now clearly evident. Also clearly evident is the anti-Christian bias of Hollywood and the networks. Is this same bias evident toward other religions, including Judaism and humanism? Absolutely not. Evidently the only religion which Hollywood and the networks consider dangerous is Christianity.

And they intend to do whatever they can to diminish Christian influence on our society.

## Results of Humanism

Rising crime, the increase in broken families, promotion of homosexuality as an approved lifestyle, cheapening of human life via abortion, etc., can, in my opinion, all be traced to the influence of the humanist religion as communicated by our national mass media. The national news and entertainment media, by their own admission, have little relationship with or respect for the church, and yet they serve as the "moral guardians" of our society. Their moral codes gain media acceptance; their moral rejections gain media condemnation. The media's anti-Christian attitude is not an accident. It is intentional. These leaders desire that their religion—humanism—replace the Christian view of man as the foundation of our society. And they use their positions of influence to achieve that desire.

What is the danger to the church and to our country in this intentional movement to restructure the foundation of our society? The danger lies not in the vulgar and obscene pictures which grace the pornographic magazines and films or explicit television programs. The danger is the philosophy behind those pictures. That philosophy, the one which the leaders of the media are pushing on the American public, is humanism.

This philosophy, in the final analysis, coincides exactly with that of Larry Flynt, publisher of *Hustler* magazine. Flynt bought full-page ads in many newspapers attacking the influence of the Christian faith in this country. (Incidentally, only a handful of papers refused to run the ads because of their anti-Christian content. No doubt all of them would have refused the ads if they were anti-Semitic or anti-black.) Many people are repulsed by Flynt and his pornography. However, his philosophy is identical to that of Hugh Hefner, the publisher of *Playboy* magazine, and Bob Guccione, publisher of *Penthouse* magazine. Hefner is the person embodying this philosophy who is most admired by leaders of the secular media. While Flynt's and Guccione's magazines are considered coarse by many who readily accept Hefner's magazine, philosophically there is no difference among the three.

To whom is this philosophy marketed? *Playboy, Penthouse, Hustler,* and all pornography is directed primarily toward teenaged to middle-aged males. Pornography is the means to sell this philosophy to the fathers and future fathers of America. This philosophy has no room for the old, the sick, the poor, the physically unlovely, the family, or the church. The fathers of tomorrow are being educated that the most important thing in life is the satisfaction of physical, sensual desires. A natural consequence of this is the dramatic rise in divorce, the growing number of homes without a father, the rise in rape and abortion, and a general cheapening of human life.

To whom is this humanist philosophy marketed on television? Most network programs are marketed toward teenaged to middle-aged women. Television is the means to sell the religion of humanism to the mothers and future mothers of America. Thus the humanist, anti-Christian philosophy is effectively marketed to young parents and future parents as the norm, the ideal!

The most effective preachers in our society aren't men like Robert Schuller, Jerry Falwell, Oral Roberts, and Billy Graham. Not by any means. The preachers most effectively using the mass media are people like Hugh Hefner, Bob Guccione, Norman Lear, and Lee

Rich. Those who oppose Christianity—often bitterly and viciously—are the ones who most effectively control the mass media.

While other segments of the mass media are not as openly hostile to the Christian faith as are Hefner, Guccione, and Flynt, they are nevertheless advocates of this same humanist philosophy. Pick up any copy of *Cosmopolitan,* or most women's or teenage girls' magazines, and check out the contents. You will find the same humanist philosophy permeating the vast majority. Rarely is the Christian view of man presented as preferred or being the norm.

### "Christian Influence Must Be Removed"

To the humanist mind and mentality, all influence of Christian faith must be removed from society. To achieve this end, the humanist feels obligated and duty-bound to use whatever methods available, particularly the media. It also means establishing humanism as the rule for law and justice in our society—the establishing of a system of law undergirded and guided by the humanist religion. What those seeking these changes cannot bring about through a popular movement, they seek to change through the influence of the media and the enforcement of law. According to George Gallup, 90 percent of the people of this country identify with the Christian faith. Realizing this, those seeking to shift the foundation of our society want laws to force their religion on the whole of society. (The laws of every society are based on some philosophy regarded by individuals responsible for the laws as being the highest good achievable for society. While not all the founding fathers of the United States were Christian, they did generally share the Christian view of morality and participated in establishing that view into law.)

This definite shifting of the foundation of our society from a Christian view of man to a humanist view naturally brings about changes. One of the most fundamental changes is that the church loses its ability to influence society. Additionally, with loss of influence comes a loss of respect. And this is precisely what the national media elite desire.

In some ways, the church has adopted the role assigned it by the media. Many church leaders have joined the media elite in constructing this new foundation for our society. Whether this has been done knowingly is a debatable question. Church leaders have been quick to speak out on media-favored issues such as civil rights, nuclear arms, etc. (An example of this can be seen in a recent meeting of the largest program board in my own denomination. Resolutions approved for submission to the General Conference, the highest body in the United Methodist Church, dealt with U.S. government and church relations in China, human rights in Central America, an update on South Africa, the Arab-Israeli conflict, the Philippines, Korea, "health and wholeness," and the elderly in the United States. Other actions by this same top-echelon board included an update on discussions with the United Auto Workers Union; asking that a letter from Adolfo Perez Esqueval of Argentina, calling on the United States to stop sending arms to Central America, be conveyed to the Council of Bishops; agreeing to send letters to insurance carriers supporting bills in the U.S. Congress to eliminate sex as a risk classification in insurance; and supporting the right of each program agency to elect its top staff executives.) This, in itself, deserves no criticism. Indeed, it is the role of the church to speak out on these issues.

But these same church leaders have been strangely silent on the very issues the media elite have been silent on—pornography, sex and violence in the media, etc. Many get the opinion that the leaders of the national secular media, who have absolutely no use for the church, are setting the agenda for the church.

Regardless of one's agreement or disagreement with my observations thus far, one fact cannot be argued: there has been virtually total silence by the church regarding the efforts of a humanist-led media to reshape society. Pornography has become a multi-billion-dollar industry; the networks have been pushing sex, violence, vulgarity, and anti-Christian themes and programs; and the organized, institutional church has not responded with any effort to combat this situation. The silence of the church in the face of this destruction of Christian morality is taking a toll in suffering, hurt, pain, brokenness, and separation.

A recent study of Minnesota's large Lutheran and Roman Catholic populations, who have traditionally been conservative in sexual morality, graphically indicated the influence of the humanist-dominated national media. The report, published by the Institute for Ecumenical and Cultural Research in Collegeville, Minnesota, stated that more than a third of those surveyed now tolerate premarital sex under special circumstances, and 17 percent of Minnesota Lutherans and Catholics refused to condemn adultery. Church historian Martin E. Marty says that these figures represent a major revolution: "In two or three decades in the Minnesotas of America, there has been more sudden change than in the previous two millenia of Christian history."

On the basis of hundreds of interviews with middle-class Americans during the past four years, a University of California sociologist at a recent national church meeting painted a scary picture of individualism (humanism) gone rampant. Robert Bellah said he found the typical attitude was: "You're responsible for yourself and no one else." Such a freedom, he stated, finds that "marriage, friends, job, community, church are all dispensable. This means the individual is absolute—'I am my own god.'"

## Why the Silence?

The silence of the church has helped desensitize countless numbers to the Christian Gospel. Many in the church have lost a sense of commitment to the Gospel, and others have given up because of this silence. (My own denomination lost 1,030,128 members between 1970 and 1980, a loss of 9.8 percent while the population was growing at a rate of 11.4 percent. Nearly every other large mainline denomination suffered similar losses.) Indeed, many are confused and bewildered as to the mission and purpose of the church.

The ironic question is, "Why the silence?" Why has the church, the body of Christ, been so silent as the humanist attacks continue to do so much harm and cause so much human suffering? Was it not God who gave us the Ten Commandments to establish a moral foundation? Was it not Christ who urged purity in His Sermon on the Mount? Was it not the Apostle Paul who told us to think on things which are good and pure and lovely? Why, for more than two decades, has the church sat on the sidelines with folded arms, ignoring the problem? Several reasons are offered.

*First, fear of the media.* According to this theory, church leaders who normally would be at the forefront in addressing similar problems are paralyzed by fear of media criticism. They are afraid that speaking out will cause the media to respond with unfavorable personal attacks. Past experience teaches that those who favor ideas favored by the media receive its blessings, while those who favor causes opposed by the media receive its wrath. Those who espouse traditional Christian values are often branded "fundamentalist," "censor," "rightwing," or some similar phrase, and often compared to Hitler, McCarthy, etc. A typical example of this is the *Washington Post's* handling of the Creationism trial in Little Rock, Arkansas. Those who favored the equal treatment of both theories of Creation were labeled by the *Post* as "impassioned believers, rebellious educators, and scientific oddities." (Their opposition, however, according to the *Post* gave "brilliant little summaries.")

*Another theory suggests that silence is the result of agreement.*

This theory holds that those who are in a position of priority-setting leadership in the various denominations are in basic agreement with the agenda and priorities set by the media. On the surface, this theory appears to have some validity.

*Third is the theory that church leaders are preoccupied with "housekeeping chores."* That is, leaders in the various denominations are so engrossed in denominational duties that they have little time or interest in dealing with the decaying morality and the media's promotion of anti-Christian values. Building buildings, raising funds, and running the denomination cause the leadership to ignore or sidestep this issue. However, this theory could, at best, be only partially correct since many leaders have joined in promoting other social issues which the media has put on the agenda.

*Fourth is the possibility that those charged with setting the agenda for various denominations don't consider this issue to be relevant.* They see it as a fundamental nonissue and do not desire their denomination to put emphasis, energy, or economics into its involvement.

*Fifth is the possibility that denominational leaders consider the saving of souls as the church's only mission.* This theory hardly carries any weight among the vast majority of denominations, however. Nearly all denominations are involved, in one way or another, with social causes beyond the saving of souls.

*Sixth, and perhaps the theory which many consider the primary one, is that leadership of the various denominations have their own "pet projects" they wish to promote and fear that addressing the promotion of anti-Christian values is a threat to those pet projects.* This theory does make some sense. Many denominations are heavily influenced by full-time "staff" people at the upper-echelon levels. These people operate somewhat in a vacuum, divorced from denominational grass-roots membership, but have tremendous power to set the agenda for their respective denominations. They see church involvement in this issue as a serious threat to the projects they personally prefer. Addressing the decline of morality would drain attention, funds, personnel, and publicity from their own projects. Therefore, they relegate this issue to the back burner for fear their pet causes will suffer.

No doubt, there are other reasons for the church's silence. One thing, however, is certain. Regardless of the reason or reasons, the church has refused to address the issue.

Some would argue that by preaching the Gospel, the church is addressing the issue, and therefore one cannot truthfully say that the church has been silent. This presumes that in preaching the Gospel the church is also addressing the problems of hunger, sickness, civil rights, nuclear arms, etc. The hypocrisy in this argument is readily evident.

## Pornography an Accepted Part of "Moral" America

The silence of the church has allowed pornography to become an accepted part of "moral" America and one of the leading sources of revenue for "respectable businesses" as well as organized crime. It has allowed television, which has the potential to be the most constructive medium in the history of mankind, to become a school for crime, immorality, and vulgarity, shaping the minds and morals of our society.

It is my opinion that the failure of the major denominations to address the declining moral situation in the country has hurt the credibility of the church more than any other single issue. I feel that the major denominations' refusal to get involved is due to the "tunnel vision" of denominational staff professionals who define social issues only in terms of civil issues. None of the issues addressed by the social agencies of the major denominations indicates a total view of the social implications of the Gospel. The professional staff people of the larger denominations have addressed social issues entirely in political and civil terms while ignoring social issues of a moral nature.

I think those responsible for setting the social agenda for most of the major denominations are narrow-minded. Their interpretation of the Gospel is entirely too shallow. If the church has no message concerning the exploitation of humans, the promotion of the theory that man is an accidental animal, and the call of man to repent of his personal sins, then the church has no message at all. My reaction to this failure is not anger, but hurt, shame, and disappointment.

At the current time, the church is losing this battle by default. And until the church decides to be the church, to assume the God-ordained responsibility to address this issue which is doing untold damage to our society, the destructive changes will continue to grow. Indeed, there is a line beyond which society can move which will mean destruction of the freedom and advancements mankind has gained in the last 2,000 years. Perhaps the line has already been crossed.

To address this issue will not be a pleasant or an easy task. Once the leaders in the national secular media perceive the church responding and posing a threat to their power and influence, they will most certainly retaliate. The church will of necessity have to learn again that suffering is a continuing essential of the Christian faith which committed believers must carry at all times in all ages.

Until the church decides to address this issue, the stories about little children suffering, such as the five young boys raped and killed by Gary Bishop, will continue to increase; pornography will continue to flourish and grow, crime will continue to rise, the family will continue to suffer, human life will become cheaper and cheaper, and the foundation of society will continue to shift from the Christian view of man to the humanist view of man. Misery and suffering will follow the refusal of the church to be the church.

I am firmly convinced that if the church fails to begin to aggressively address this situation within the next five years, then the Christian era will be over.

Many powerful people in key positions of influence in the media are intent on ridding our society of any effective Christian influence. There are basically five steps of regression in ridding our society of Christian influence: (1) ignore the church and censor it as an integral part of our society; (2) question the church and present one-sided arguments belittling it; (3) attack the church verbally; (4) ostracize from the mainstream of society those who would overtly practice their faith; and (5) physically persecute those who would practice their Christian faith.

Ostracizing Christians from the mainstream of society is just beginning. It is my belief that unless committed Christians get involved, and get involved quickly, physical persecution is only a generation away.

In the face of this onslaught of humanism from the media, the church has been like Peter. We have denied the Lord and turned our back on Him. Indeed, we should hang our heads in shame at our failure. But also like Peter, Christ gives us another opportunity. I pray that the church will respond as Peter did with the second opportunity.

Perhaps we need once again to hear the words of Christ: "Blessed are ye, when men shall revile you, and persecute you, and shall say all manner of evil against you falsely, for My sake. Rejoice, and be exceeding glad: for great is your reward in heaven: for so persecuted they the prophets which were before you" (Matt. 5:11-12).

Which will it be? Silence or taking a stand? God have mercy on us, our children, and grandchildren if the choice is continued silence.

## DISCUSSION AND REFLECTION QUESTIONS

1. Do you feel there is any connection between pornography and sex crimes?
2. Did the statistics in the studies on the various media elites surprise you?
3. Why do you think the various media elite are predominantly Jewish?
4. Are you surprised that the TV and movie elite strongly feel that TV entertainment programs should be used to reshape society?
5. The author says that the media's anti-Christian attitude is not an accident. Do you agree? Why or why not?
6. Why are people like Hugh Hefner so esteemed by the entertainment media?
7. Do you agree with the author that producers such as Norman Lear are the leading preachers using television to proclaim their message?
8. Do you feel that church leaders have adopted the values of the media more than the media have adopted the values of the church?
9. Are the top leaders in the various denominations afraid to speak out on media immorality?
10. Do you agree with the author that the church is losing the battle by default?
11. Do you agree with the author's five steps of ridding our society of Christian influence?
12. Do you agree with the author that if the church fails to begin to aggressively address the moral situation within the next five years, we will enter a post-Christian era?

# THREE

# CHANGE IS NO ACCIDENT

It is no accident that our country is the most violent country in the world. It is no accident that in our country during the past seven years more than eight million unborn babies—the weakest, most helpless, most innocent, most defenseless of all human life—have been killed. It is no accident that the divorce rate and the breakup of families in our nation has skyrocketed during the past generation and that nearly one of every two marriages will end in divorce. It is no accident that the existence of the family—the backbone to any civilized society—as the central unit in our society is now threatened. It is no accident that teenage pregnancies have become a national concern. It is no accident that we are afraid to walk the streets of our cities at night. It is no accident that we lock our homes not only at night but during the day also, or that each of us keeps our car keys in our pocket or purse when not driving.

Years ago a Jewish tentmaker spoke an eternal truth: "Whatsoever a man soweth, that shall he also reap" (Gal. 6:7). That truth is as valid for a nation as it is for an individual. Truth cannot be avoided. Truth cannot be changed. Truth cannot be manipulated. Even when it is crushed to earth, it will rise again.

The truth of the words of Paul of Tarsus is evident in our country today. For more than a generation, our society has been sowing seeds which are today bringing forth their fruit.

No, things don't just happen. One of the most elementary of all scientific truths is the law of cause and effect. Things are caused to happen. Put a lighted match in an empty gasoline can and you will have an explosion. It is a scientific, undeniable truth. Truth is as much a part of the makeup of man as it is the environment in which man lives. Teach a child to cheat to secure his goal, and he will do so until he is taught otherwise.

For a generation, our society has been taught, subtly but effectively, that one's religious faith is a personal and private matter and should not interfere with one's daily living. The chairman of the board of one of the largest companies in America, a company whose sales run in the billions annually and which employs nearly 100,000 people, wrote me the following: "The Ten Commandments and the Sermon on the Mount are vanished Americanisms and the situation is moving from bad to worse except, as you know, there is a core of very religious people who are becoming more fervent and active in their religion—probably as a reaction to the evil they find around them."

For nearly 200 years, our country has been guided by a strong reliance on God. Every president, from Washington to Reagan, took his oath of office with his hand on a Bible. That is not to say that all Americans were religious people in the traditional sense. Indeed, they were not. Freedom of religion also meant freedom from religion and many availed themselves of that opportunity and still do. But underneath the heart of America there was a strong and abiding belief in the guiding hand of a Divine Being. Today that belief appears to be slowly dying, pushed aside by individuals whose religion is self-interest and self-indulgence.

In its place has arisen an anti-Christian attitude which no one dared to predict a generation ago. So strong is this anti-Christian attitude that in today's moral climate it would be impossible for Congress to make Christmas a legal holiday; to place "In God We Trust" on our coins; to include in the Pledge of Allegiance the phrase "One nation, under God"; to have a chaplain open each session of Congress with a prayer; or even to allow our armed services to have chaplains. If we attempted to institute these things today, they would not survive the thinking stage.

Humanism may not be the official religion of our country, but it has become the accepted practical religion by many in key positions of influence. The liberty dreamed by our forefathers and written into our Constitution has become for many a license. Liberty used as a license will not long exist. Freedom without responsibility is self-destructive.

It comes as no surprise that this situation has created a conflict in our society of which we are only seeing the beginning, a conflict which will grow in intensity and become more bitter and more acute as time passes. What else should we expect? Humanism and Christianity are natural enemies. Most of the people in this country claim to be Christian. A conflict between those people and anti-Christian philosophies was and is inevitable.

I find it odd, yet revealing, that many of those who want to save the baby seal find nothing wrong with killing the unborn, innocent human baby. I find it odd, yet revealing, that many of those who are concerned about air pollution and water pollution will contribute generously to mind pollution. When Hugh Hefner made a contribution to the National Organization of Women, it was a hypocritical gesture of the highest magnitude, topped only by NOW's act of accepting it.

I find it odd that a fourteen-year-old must have her parents' permission to have her ears pierced, but not to have an abortion. I find it no accident that those who desire to have no-morals sex education taught in the public schools are the same people who tell parents to turn off their television set if the programs are teaching sexual immorality. I find it odd that our government will give a fifteen-year-old contraceptives without the permission or knowledge of her parents, but that same fifteen-year-old must have a parent's permission to take a school field trip.

It is no accident that the public schools in our nation—long a backbone for a strong country—are struggling, while private, Christian schools—long struggling—are growing at a record rate. Caring parents want their children not only to learn to read, write, and do arithmetic, but also to learn basic Judeo-Christian moral values such as honesty, fairness, politeness, patriotism, integrity, discipline, obedience to authority, and kindness. And they want the education to take place in an atmosphere of Judeo-Christian moral conduct.

## Greatest Threat Is Mind Pollution

The greatest threat to the existence of our society today is not air pollution or water pollution, but mind pollution. For the first time in history, man has an instrument through which the masses can be taught effectively, immediately, and effortlessly. That instrument is television. To deny that television is a teacher and a motivator is to deny reality. Businessmen do not make cold, hard business decisions based on a theory that television sells. They *know* television sells. And based on that fact, they spend more than thirteen billion dollars each year selling their products via television. But television sells more than products—it sells ideas, concepts, values, morals, and those other intangibles which affect the life of every person. To allow this wonderful medium of television to be used to line the financial pockets of a few at the expense of the masses is a terrible tragedy.

Neither should network and Hollywood officials think that Christian people will passively sit by while their faith is ignored, ridiculed, or belittled. When Harvard University said that 70 percent of all allusions to sexual intercourse on television were between people not married to each other or involved a prostitute, it was simply confirming the fact that Hollywood and the networks were needlessly ridiculing our faith.

As Christians, we are concerned not only by what Hollywood and the networks make available to us, but also by what they fail to show. A chaplain in New York State sent me a copy of a letter he had mailed to Universal Television. "Last evening I watched an excellent performance of 'Quincy' on NBC. The program was about a young woman dying of cancer who wanted to die with dignity but was encountering opposition from her husband. Dr. Quincy and a psychiatrist dealt with the emotional problems involved. I have one question. I have worked in three general hospitals as a chaplain. In none of these hospitals was a psychiatrist on the staff, but chaplains were. Also, the pathologists on the staff were never involved in the emotional and personal problems of the patients but simply performed their pathological duties. However, chaplains were regularly involved in these problems. This is their function. I therefore ask why the reluctance to present the clergy or religion when appropriate on TV? A chaplain would have been much more appropriate than a pathologist or psychiatrist in the program last evening. The religious dimension is a vital aspect of life. Why the hesitancy to present it as such?" Yes, why censor Christians and other religious characters from TV programs?

When Lee Rich, producer of "Dallas," "Flamingo Road," and other programs, said that he had not been to church since he was seventeen (he is now about sixty) and that he did not know a single person who went to church (and he mixes and mingles with those who are responsible for what we see everyday and knows them on a first-name basis), it answered a lot of questions about why television ignores or belittles Christian values. That there should be a conflict between the networks and Hollywood and the Christian community should not come as a surprise. It was inevitable.

Among the most notable and visible producers in Hollywood is Norman Lear, founder of People for the American Way. While he has been very critical of ministers who speak out on social issues, I feel it should be noted that Lear hired Virginia Carter, described by

e magazine as "a fervent feminist and a passionate liberal,"
gave her the task of working her favorite social issues into
,odes of his programs. She admitted she and Lear used the pro-
ams to advocate positions. "I consider it a duty to serve as an
advocate," Carter said. "To waste that valuable airspace I'd have to
be crazy." And while Lear complains about ministers who have access to one or two million viewers a week, he fails to note that the
National Association of Better Broadcasting stated in 1976 that Lear
"talks" by television "to more people each week than any other
person in history." At one time as many as fifteen million man
hours each week were spent watching Lear's programs, listening to
his social "sermons." Lear's method of "talking" in his programs
is simply another way of "preaching," as Virginia Carter so well
noted.

## How Does Mr. Lear Use Television?
A newspaper article by Mary Beth Murphy described how Norman
Lear uses television to preach. "He walked to the podium and was
greeted by a pleasant, rather mild round of applause. . . . The symposium was sponsored by Action for Children's Television. 'Thank
you for that warm and generous welcome, although it was not as
warm and generous as I like it.' With that he proceeded to motivate
the audience into giving him a 'spontaneous' cheering, madly ap-
plauding welcome. As an added incentive for the audience, he pointed out that he was taping the talk and was going to edit the tape so
that when his name was mentioned, the second madly 'spontaneous'
outburst would be heard. . . . 'I just manipulated you,' Lear said
with a smile. The TV hit-maker just did an abbreviated version of
what his shows do to audiences weekly—send a message wrapped in
humor. . . . 'People,' he said, 'accept information more readily when
they're being entertained.' "
What kind of information has Norman Lear been preaching? On
"The Nancy Walker Show," one of the leading characters remarked:
"Just because a man yields to the temptation of lust doesn't mean he
loves his wife less." And on "All in the Family," Archie's coworker
asked: "What's wrong with a married man having somebody stashed
away somewhere?" Remember that Lear said people accept information more readily when they are being entertained.
On "Maude," there was an episode on wife-swapping entitled
"Maude's New Friends" (a psychiatrist and his wife). The psychiatrist
suggested that the two couples swap wives and said to Maude: "I
want to go to bed with you." Lear said people accept information

more readily when they are being entertained.

On "Mary Hartman, Mary Hartman," Wanda and Lila had a lesbian affair while Merle slept with both. On one program, Wanda told Merle: "That's what marriage is, concentrated lust." On another program, Mary, who was married to Tom, made love to Dennis in his hospital bed. On still another, Kathy, unwed and pregnant, was talking with Grandpa and admitted that she was the "pushover of Fernwood." Grandpa assured her: "You're sweet, you're kind, and you're fun. These are the things that count, not how many affairs you have had." Lear said people accept information more readily when they are being entertained.

On another "Nancy Walker" episode, Nancy's husband was reluctant to try marijuana, wondering if it might lead to an evil habit. Nancy told him not to worry, because "evil" spelled backward is "live." Lear said people accept information more readily when they are being entertained.

Lear quite often has something to say about Christians and Christianity, hardly any of it positive. On "All in the Family," Archie wanted to have his new grandson baptized. When the child's parents would not go along with his suggestion, Archie decided to have the sacrament performed without their permission. When Edith objected, Archie said: "You gotta use force; that is the Christian way." Lear said people accept information more readily when they are being entertained.

On "Mary Hartman, Mary Hartman," Lear ridiculed the passion and death of Christ. One character, Rev. Jimmy Joe, an eight-year-old evangelist, died when the television set fell into his bathtub while he was watching a news report about a plane crashing into a church. Comparing Jimmy Joe to Christ, Loretta said: "He died for the 6:30 news, Lord. For the sins of the 6:30 news." Lear said people accept information more readily when they are being entertained.

Lear, the gentleman who espouses "pluralism," called the people of Peoria, Illinois "provincial" when they supported their television station's decision not to air his controversial "Maude" abortion episodes.

Lear finds it acceptable for some groups to use force to change television in their own mold. Speaking about Action for Children's Television, he said: "They forced their way on the networks. They forced the networks to be attentive. . . . They've done that in the healthiest manner that is totally consistent with the spirit of liberty in this country." But he has been very critical of many Christians for practicing one of the most fundamental rights afforded us, the privilege of boycotting advertisers who help sponsor the programs.

## Boycotting Is Not Censorship but Stewardship

In March 1982, the Coalition for Better Television asked Christians and other concerned individuals to begin boycotting RCA products and Hertz car and truck rentals because of the violence, vulgarity, and anti-Christian programming on NBC. NBC is owned by RCA, as is Hertz.

That boycott of RCA/NBC is an exercise of stewardship, not censorship. The accusation that the boycott is censorship makes as much sense as NBC entertainment president Brandon Tartikoff's charge that the boycott was "the first step toward a police state. . . ." Tartikoff seems to think that the republic will fall unless we continue to financially support what many of us feel is offensive and destructive programming. Our republic existed long before television turned to vulgar and violent programming. The question Tartikoff should ask himself is how long the republic can stand when given a steady diet of adultery, murder, profanity, drinking, drug use, and mockery of Christianity on network television.

We are left with the opinion from the networks that we are under an obligation to support that which we find to be morally offensive or mentally insulting. We are not. Christian support of vulgar or tasteless programming is no more our obligation than it is an obligation of the United States to economically support the Soviet government.

What is it about me that is objectionable to the networks and Hollywood? They say they object to my methods, methods that encourage people to practice selective buying as well as selective viewing. But that reply is intentionally deceitful. It isn't my methods they find objectionable. No. If it were my methods, they would have criticized other organizations which use the same methods. For instance, when the NAACP (National Association for the Advancement of Colored People) threatened to boycott films that did not use blacks behind and in front of the camera, there was no righteous repudiation coming forth from New York and Hollywood. No charges of censorship or police state beginnings. But when the Coalition for Better Television declared its boycott, *The Hollywood Reporter's* front-page headlines screamed in big, bold, black headlines: "Rev. Wildmon on the Rampage Again: New Boycott Threatened."

When NAACP head Benjamin Hooks threatened a boycott, there

were no headlines which read: "Benjamin Hooks on the Rampage Again: New Boycott Threatened." When the Directors Guild of America announced its boycott of states which had not ratified the ERA, there were no big headlines calling the boycott unfair or repressive.

When the Oral Majority announced a boycott of Procter & Gamble because of that company's withdrawal from fifty programs they found unsuitable for their ads, there were no holy cries of censorship, no headlines which read: "Homosexuals on Rampage Again." No, it is not my methods to which the networks and Hollywood object. They have proven that. What, then, is it?

Gene Mater, vice-president of policy, CBS-TV, revealed my objectionable quality in a debate we had in Los Angeles. When I asked Mater why it was right for other groups, including homosexuals, to do the same thing I was doing, he replied: "The difference—I think what sets you apart . . . your organization apart . . . is the fact that you are . . . cloaked in this self-assumed aura of religious respectability." Therein lies the problem. It is not my methods but my ideas that represent a threat. Which ideas? Ideas which spring directly from my Christian faith. That is what the networks and Hollywood find dangerous.

So, then, it is my ideas which must be suppressed. Ideas, you see, can be dangerous. While the networks accuse the coalition and myself of censorship, they are practicing that of which they accuse us. They censor the ideas I espouse, ideas which spring directly from my Christian faith, because they find these ideas dangerous.

## These Ideas Have Been Dangerous for Centuries
This is nothing new. These ideas I hold have been dangerous for 2,000 years. They were so dangerous that the Person to first advocate them ended up on a cross, crucified by the power brokers of His day. Ideas so dangerous that for nearly 300 years the Roman Empire threatened to kill and indeed did kill those who held them. Ideas so dangerous that in Soviet Russia in this century more than twelve million people have been put to death because they have held them (a fact one would never learn watching network news). Ideas so dangerous that Hollywood and the networks find they must be suppressed and censored.

What are these ideas which Hollywood and the networks oppose? To begin with, the idea that man is more than an animal, that man is created in the image of God. That, indeed, is a dangerous idea. Let a person begin to conceive of himself as being infinitely important,

image of the Creator of the earth, and he behaves
becomes a new creature. He seeks a better way. He
ation and greed.

of dangerous ideas do I have? The idea that says sex is
d-given gift to be shared between husband and wife,
cheap and vulgar like the networks and Hollywood
make it. That is a dangerous idea. Should it be allowed to catch
hold, then all the pornographers and many of the filmmakers would
suffer monetary loss.

What kinds of ideas? The idea that says violence is not God's way
of resolving conflict. Surely that is a dangerous idea. Allowed to
spread, the public might reject the steady diet of violence on the
screen and in the news. The job of Hollywood and the networks
would thus be complicated. Some imagination, creativity, and objec-
tivity might be necessary.

What kinds of ideas do I hold that are dangerous? The idea that
the elderly are an important part of society, to be honored and
respected for their wisdom and experience. That is dangerous. The
networks and Hollywood depend on youth, primarily female youth,
which they can exploit. To see beauty as something intrinsic, rather
than meat well-proportioned on human bones, is dangerous. Writers
might have to use creativity and imagination to bring forth suitable
scripts. Presenting a half-naked female would no longer be considered art. Females might have to be treated as intelligent humans
instead of sex objects.

What kinds of ideas? The idea that says intelligent and thoughtful
people can express themselves without resorting to vulgar, crude,
and filthy language. That is dangerous. If Hollywood and the networks should ever have to face that idea from the public, they would
have to use skill to get across a forceful point.

What kinds of ideas? The idea that says illegal drugs should be
presented from a negative light, shown as nonapproved behavior and
detrimental to the well-being of the individual and society. The idea
that says alcohol should not be the overwhelming drink on television; and when it is shown, the results of alcohol should also be
shown—deaths on the highways, deaths and violence in the home,
lost production, human suffering. Those, indeed, are dangerous
ideas.

What kinds of ideas? The idea that capitalism, nurtured by Christian ethics, is the finest economic system ever devised by mankind.
This idea is so rejected by Hollywood that Jim Brooks, a television
writer and former producer of "The Mary Tyler Moore Show," said

concerning businessmen: "They are all sons-of-bi___. They're cannibals." Douglas Benton, another successful writer and producer, put forth his idea of capitalism nurtured by Christian ethics. "We are inevitably moving toward socialism. Ultimately it will come to socialism, because it's the only governmental organization which attempts to take care of the dumb and the weak and the helpless. The free enterprise system is set up to reward your energy." The Media Institute released a study which reported 67 percent of businessmen are depicted on television in a negative way and reported: "Fully three quarters of those corporate leaders portrayed in a negative light engage in illegal activity. . . . Over half of all business leaders on those prime-time shows . . . are portrayed as criminals." It is the capitalistic system, nurtured by Christian ethics, that has made America the richest, most prosperous country in all the world and has allowed us, more than any other country in history, to help the underprivileged countries of the world. Capitalism, divorced from Christian ethics, will become a most callous economic system, more socially repressive than Communism.

What kinds of ideas do I hold that are dangerous? The idea that religion is a vital part of life; that according to George Gallup, 90 percent of Americans consider themselves Christian and that more than fifty million people attend worship services regularly. That the Christian faith has helped build schools and hospitals, house the homeless, feed the hungry, heal the broken home, restore the alcoholic, and play a vital and central role in making this country the greatest on earth. To the networks, that is a dangerous idea, so dangerous they do not allow it to be shown.

So it isn't my methods the networks and Hollywood reject. They have approved the same methods for others. It is my ideas (my concept of man) that are dangerous. They must not let these dangerous ideas spread. They may be contagious.

## What Is at Stake?

What is at stake in all of this goes far beyond sex and violence on television. What is at stake here is whether we will remain a country that accepts the Judeo-Christian concept of right and wrong, or turn our backs on centuries of progress to embrace practical atheism. The kind of society our children and our children's children will live in is at stake. Our nation will reap what we sow. That is a truth you can deposit and draw interest on.

We can have a society that recognizes God and His moral standards, or we can have a godless society which recognizes the with no absolute morals or values. We cannot, ...oth as equals. We cannot have a society where we ...an life as both precious and a convenience.

...e our law and justice, our determination of right and ...e Christian view of man, or we can base our law and ...determination of right and wrong, on the humanist valu... Hollywood and the networks. But we cannot have our base on both because they are diametrically opposed to each other.

Whether we reject God or affirm Him, the fact remains that we are still brothers together in the family of man. We can follow the negative example of Cain in dealing with our brothers, or we can follow the positive example of Andrew, who was concerned for Simon Peter's spiritual welfare; but we are, always have been, and always will be brothers.

We have seen the changes which have taken place in our nation in the last generation. Is ours a safer, better, more moral, more stable society than it was a generation ago? Is the quality of life better than it was a generation ago? And if crime, drug use, divorces, abortions on demand, pornography, apathy, and similar social ills continue for another generation as they have in the past generation, will we have the kind of society in which we want our grandchildren to grow up? Do we desire to proceed in the same direction morally which we have been going for the past quarter of a century? Are we ready to sell our national soul for a mess of valueless pottage? I certainly hope not.

The greatest resource America has is her people. The most precious gift in all the world is human life. The greatest good is to serve our fellowman. The greatest tragedy is our refusal to get involved on behalf of those who will come after us. A nation which turns its back on God and His moral standards will reap what it sows. That was true 2,000 years ago. It is true today. It will be true 2,000 years from now even if we reject it.


## DISCUSSION AND REFLECTION QUESTIONS

1. Do you agree with the author that the changes which have occured in American society are not accidents but the direct result of influences exerted on our society?

2. Do you think that the phrase "In God We Trust" could be placed on our coins today if it were not already there?

3. Do you agree that humanism and Christianity are natural enemies?

4. Does television, in news reporting and entertainment programs, try to manipulate viewers?

5. Do you feel people such as Norman Lear have made our society a better place in which to live, work, and raise a family through the social messages in their programs?

6. Is boycotting sponsors of violent, vulgar, and anti-Christian programs a valid expression of Christian stewardship? Why or why not?

7. Do you agree with the author that the networks objected to his ideas more than his methods?

8. Do you agree with the ideas to which the author says the networks objected?

9. Should our system of law and justice be based on the Christian view of man or on the humanist view of man? For what reasons?

10. Is our society, overall, a better, safer, more moral, more stable, and just society than it was thirty years ago?

# FOUR

# THE BATTLE IS INTERNAL

We Americans are caught up in a great struggle unlike any which we have faced before. Our struggle is not with an enemy from beyond our shores as it has been in the past; it is being waged inside our very borders. The outcome will determine the direction our country will take for the next several centuries.

This great struggle is one of values—particularly which ones will be the standard for our society and a base for our system of justice in the years to come. For 200 years our country has based its morals, its sense of right and wrong, on the Christian view of man. The Ten Commandments and the Sermon on the Mount have been our solid foundation. To be sure, we have never managed to get the system perfect in practice. Nor will we ever be able to do so regardless of what base we use. But it has been the most perfect system ever devised in the history of mankind.

Today there are those who would have us change; go in new directions; directions, they are convinced, that will free man from his chains of oppression. They are tired of this old system. They want a new one. And the new one will be based on what they perceive to be right and wrong. The standards for society will come from within themselves. They will decide for themselves and, consequently, for society what kinds of conduct are acceptable and unacceptable. The old Christian morals will be cast aside in pursuit of a new society.

Had anyone said to me seven years ago that I would be writing this, I would have told him he was crazy. In fact, if someone had said to me seven years ago what I now believe to be true, I would have tried my best to avoid him. Why? Because in my eyes he would have been a fanatic. And none of us desire to listen to a fanatic.

If someone had told me seven years ago that our country was in the midst of a great struggle, a struggle which would determine the kind of society we would have for generations to come, I would have laughed at him. But we are. And I shall not fault anyone who desires to laugh at me.

If within the next five years we fail to turn the tide of this humanist value system which seeks to replace our Christian heritage, then we have—in my opinion—lost the struggle and it will be generations, if at all, before the Christian view of man will be the norm again. I don't like making such a statement. But I must write what I perceive to be the truth.

As a young minister I remember how cold chills ran over my body when I discovered what happened to unwanted babies in Rome at the time of Christ. They were thrown into the sewer! And even in enlightened Athens unwanted children were discarded in the woods for the animals to eat. I thought about how much we have changed since then, how civilized we have become, how much more compassionate we are today than 2,000 years ago. Then I am told that every year there are more than one million abortions in this country. We haven't changed that much. We wouldn't dare throw a baby into the sewer. Today we kill babies in the sterile atmosphere of a modern hospital or an abortion clinic and put the bodies in trash bags for disposal in garbage bins. It is so respectable that we even allocate tax money to help cover the expense. We aren't more civilized, only more efficient in our cruelty. Jesus' words, "Suffer the little children to come unto Me," seem out of place in this new society.

### Television, the Greatest Educator in Our Society

Television is the most pervasive and persuasive medium we have. At times it is larger than life. It is our only true national medium. Network television is the greatest educator we have. It tells us, in its programming, what is right and wrong, what is acceptable and unacceptable, whom to believe and not to believe, whom to trust and not trust, and whom we should desire to emulate. In one interview, most teenage boys said they wanted to be like Burt Reynolds! The medium sold them.

We speak of educational television as if it is a separate channel. Not only is PBS educational television, but so are CBS, NBC, and ABC. All television is educational. That being true, what is it teaching?

It is teaching that adultery is an acceptable and approved lifestyle.

It is teaching that violence is a legitimate way to achieve one's goals or to resolve conflict. It is teaching that profanity is the language of the respectable. But these are only surface messages. The real message is deeper.

It is teaching that hardly anyone goes to church, that very few people in our society are Christian or live by Christian principles. How? By simply censoring Christian characters, Christian values, and Christian culture from the programs. It is teaching that people who claim to be Christian are hypocrites, cheats, liars, or worse. It does so by characterization.

In the NBC production, *The Word,* a character played by Geraldine Chaplin announced to the hero, David Janssen: "I'm the former Sister Mary of the Angels" and shortly thereafter lives with him. She reasoned, "I keep my body and soul separate—you have my body for one night; Jesus has my soul forever."

One episode of "The Rockford Files" portrayed a young woman's rather ridiculous journey through the world of rolfing, primal scream, and the local ashram, until she reached what the producers evidently thought was her logical destination: passing out tracts on a street corner. An ad for "Hawaii Five-O" read: "Phony preacher spreads a gospel of sin! Armed assault and a violent death put McGarrett on the trail of a fraudulent evangelist who seduces his female parishioners and fleeces them of their savings!" An ad for "Lou Grant" asked: "Is a dynamic preacher keeping the faith—or keeping the money? A psychotic churchgoer leads Lou to investigate a cult's secrets. Are they praying—or being preyed upon?"

In the ABC movie, *The Cracker Factory,* the Christian faith of the protagonist's husband was presented as a major reason for her drinking and depression. In one scene where the priest visited the lady at the mental hospital, he was presented as a fanatic who cared about nothing but a hardline approach to the teaching of the church.

NBC's "Saturday Night Live" had a skit entitled "Jesus in Blue Jeans." One of the songs advertised and sung was entitled "Yummy, Yummy, Yummy, I've Got God in My Tummy" while a picture of the Last Supper was on the screen.

In one episode of "Police Story," a man and his son-in-law made a practice of robbing and raping young waitresses. While the rapes were in progress, the wives of the two men, mother and daughter, sat in a car, calmly waiting. To pass the time, they prayed and read the Bible.

In "Mary Hartman, Mary Hartman" (a Norman Lear production),

Loretta, portrayed as utterly ignorant and stupid, but equally sincere and well-intentioned, was chosen to represent the Christian person concerned with the salvation of souls. In that same program, Merle exploited his son's evangelistic-work-for-profit. He was involved in some sort of shady housing deal called "Condos for Christ." After the boy's death, Merle planned to devote all his time to this semiswindle while talking about "spreading the message of Christ." The Rev. Mr. Steadfast (that was his name), another character on the show, carried a pint of whiskey in a hollowed-out Bible, had an affair with his female choir director, and had to be blackmailed before he would help get Mary away from a mass murderer who was holding her hostage.

Also on "Mary Hartman, Mary Hartman," Mary explained that the presence of so many Bibles around the Hartman house was due to the fact that her sister, Kathy, met her gentlemen friends in various hotels. She always brought home a Gideon Bible from each of her "visits." It was Norman Lear's way of ridiculing those who believe in the commandments "Thou shalt not commit adultery" and "Thou shalt not steal." Sacred religious principles are always good for a disparaging laugh.

If I have learned anything about television in the past seven years I have learned this: nothing on television is there by accident. Everything is there by design and for a purpose. Others have noticed it too.

One lady wrote: "In *East of Eden,* the madam of a prostitution house is wearing a large, obvious cross or crucifix." Get the message? Another writer told about a "Saturday Night Live" program. "It is with anger and disgust that I describe the 'Babies in Makeup' movie clip. To the best of my ability, this is what I recall. A sleeping baby with the camera moving slowly up the legs to highlight bare buttocks with a red arrow painted on one cheek. Camera moved slowly upward to the face which was grotesquely made up (like punk rock). Blocks spelled out 'Babies in Makeup.' All of the children were made up in a bizarre manner. The ages ranged from about six months to approximately two and a half years. One child was dressed in black tights and had a *crucifix or cross* hung around his neck. Another child in black tights had a black whip in hand" (italics mine).

That program also prompted a call to me from an independent producer in suburban Washington who was really upset. United Press International (UPI) said the program "toddled at the very edge of kiddie porn and may have been saved from going over only by the fact that the segment was a mercifully scant thirty seconds in length."

Here is a review of the CBS movie, *Carrie*: "A withdrawn teenager lives in a ramshackle house with a religiously fanatic, sexually repressed mother." At the end of the movie, the show's only Christian—the religiously fanatic, sexually repressed mother—talks to her daughter about the daughter's father. "I should have killed myself after he took me, before we were married." She remembers "the sin" she and her husband committed—drinking, sex, etc. "And I was weak and backsliding. . . . We will pray . . . pray . . . pray . . . for the last time we will pray," says the mother. She then takes Carrie in her arms and stabs the girl. The mother then walks around Carrie and, holding the knife high, begins to stab her again. Carrie uses her demonic power to cause knives to come off the wall and stab her mother.

Several knives are shown sticking in the mother. The house then caves in, catches fire, and burns. The scene then shows a picture of Jesus with knives stuck in Him. The movie ends with a "For Sale" sign in the form of a cross in the front yard which reads: "Carrie White Burns in Hell."

### Jesus Betraying Judas?

Listen to what Peter J. Boyer, former Associated Press (AP) television writer, had to say about the CBS production, *The Day Christ Died*: "And now comes *The Day Christ Died*, a CBS film that seems almost calculated to stir a brouhaha. To say that *The Day Christ Died* departs from the traditional telling of the Easter story is to brazenly understate the matter.

"This isn't a religious story, it's a political intrigue caper. . . . Judas is no cheap traitor here, selling his Lord for thirty pieces of silver. Indeed, Judas Iscariot, the man whose name came to mean treachery itself, was a political activist whose ideals prompted his actions. *If anything, this movie suggests Christ betrayed Judas.* . . . Judas, you see, was a dedicated patriot who'd been sold out by his leader" (italics mine).

Seldom do you see a Christmas program dealing with the birth of Jesus Christ and what that birth meant to the world. Rarely is there ever a hint of anything "Christian" about Christmas. It was no accident that RCA/NBC used Christmas to feature the Playboy "playmates" on their "George Burns Early, Early, Early Christmas Program." It seemed the natural thing to do. Use the birthday of Christ, one of the most sacred days of the year for Christians, to promote a hedonistic philosophy diametrically opposed to Christianity.

*The Day Christ Died* ended with the Crucifixion. There was no Resurrection. You might be interested in knowing that Edward Anhalt, the man selected by CBS to write the script, is a self-professed agnostic. He said of Jim Bishop, the man who wrote the book on which the program was supposedly based: "First, I don't think Jim Bishop understands his own religion. Second, I never read the book. And third, if Jim Bishop thinks I have blasphemed, then I think Jim Bishop is full of ___." Bishop was so upset with CBS's distortion of the truth of the Gospels and his research that he asked that his name be removed and not associated with the program.

In one episode of "Welcome Back, Kotter," a teenage girl said that she was pregnant and that one of the "sweathogs" was responsible. All the boys denied it. Somebody suggested: "We should put a candle in the window because the last time this happened three wise men came from the East."

And on "All's Fair" (another Norman Lear program), when the pregnant Charley refused Richard's proposal of marriage, he asked: "Are you telling me this baby is going to be born without a father?" Charley answered: "No, that happened only once."

Only a relatively small handful of people determine what Americans can and will see on network television. These people are overtly hostile to the Christian faith.

We need not apologize for being Christian or for seeking to raise our families in a society directed by Christian principles and values. We must get involved and be willing to take the criticism which will be aimed at us.

Much has been said in the press about the Coalition for Better Television, which I head. Let me state the premise on which the coalition works and then you decide if it's a rightwing, fundamentalist, censorship group.

Here is the premise: The networks can show what they desire to show; the advertiser can sponsor what he desires to sponsor; the viewer can watch any of the options made available to him by the networks (and it is the networks and only the networks who tell you what you can and cannot watch); and the consumer can spend his money where he desires.

For following that pure rule of democratic capitalism, the networks compare me to Hitler, McCarthy, and Khomeini. I am called a censor without asking for a single law to be passed. I am accused of trying to dictate what the networks can show, what topics can and cannot be explored, all without having any power at the networks whatsoever. Because I care, am concerned, and because I am expressing my concern in a time-honored manner compatible with the democratic, free enterprise, capitalistic system which goes back to the early colonies, I am held up to ridicule and false accusations by the networks and bigoted remarks by some network professionals. For doing nothing more than being true to my faith, I am the object of a vicious, slurring, anti-Christian remark by James Rosenfield, president of CBS, who called me the "ayatollah of the religious right."

I hope the church will assume its God-appointed responsibility in this great battle. If it fails to do so, we will abandon more than 200 years of Christian heritage and replace it with a humanist value system determined by a small group of people who mock and belittle those who choose to follow One who hung on a cross to show us the Way.

## DISCUSSION AND REFLECTION QUESTIONS

1. Do you agree with the author that we're in the midst of a great struggle to determine the values that will guide society?
2. Are people who are concerned about the moral situation in our society generally presented by the media as being "fanatics" or "extremists"?
3. What is the difference between abortion on demand and the throwing of unwanted babies into the sewers of Rome?
4. Is the author correct in his assumption as to what television is teaching?
5. Why do you think Christians and Christianity are continually ridiculed, demeaned, and negatively stereotyped on television?
6. Are other religions treated in a negative manner by the media?
7. Do the networks take liberties and change Scripture to make programs fit their own preconceived ideas of biblical events?
8. Must Christians be willing to risk media criticism by getting involved to work for changes?
9. Is the premise of the Coalition for Better Television in keeping with democracy and Christianity?
10. Were you aware that a relatively small number of people control what one can watch on the networks?

# FIVE

# ANTI-CHRISTIAN STEREOTYPING

It was not easy for me to use the term "anti-Christian" regarding network television. It took a year of study before I was willing to do so. But much of network programming is viciously anti-Christian. This anti-Christian hostility is reflected in two ways: (1) censoring any positive portrayal of Christians in a modern-day setting; (2) presenting modern-day Christians, nearly without exception, in a negative manner.

The common media stereotype of the Christian as a narrow-minded, self-righteous, judgmental character occurred in the CBS movie, *Mark, I Love You*. The story revolves around Hal Painter, a widower with a young son (Mark), and his struggle to regain custody of his son from the boy's "Christian" maternal grandparents (Dwight and Margaret Bannister).

Following the death of his wife and daughter, Hal leaves young Mark with the Bannisters on their Iowa farm while he returns to California, hoping to find employment and "get himself together."

From this point forward, the two main adult males—Hal and Dwight—are developed in a clear-cut hero-villain relationship. The hero is Hal. He captures the hearts of viewers with his warm, loving, sensitive, and honest nature. He claims to be nothing but himself. At one point, Hal is shown in bed with Marilyn (whom he later marries), but the movie in no way suggests that this is inappropriate. Hal sincerely tries to follow due process to win back his son.

The villain is Dwight, Mark's grandfather. He and the grandmother conspire to gain custody of the boy. Dwight is a Sunday School teacher and tells of trying to bring Mark up right by taking him to Sunday School. Yet Dwight is the character you love to hate. He is arrogant, intolerant, self-righteous, and dishonest. He is angry, vindictive, and judgmental. In his attempt to gain custody of Mark, he distorts and twists the truth. He even pays off a witness.

When Hal meets Marilyn, he calls the Bannisters and Mark to tell them that he and Marilyn may get married.

HAL: May I speak to Mark?

DWIGHT: No, uh, no. He's gone to the grocery with Margaret.

HAL: (As he speaks, Margaret walks through the door, drying dishes—obviously not at the grocery.) Will you have him call me when he gets back, collect? I have a surprise for him.

DWIGHT: Oh? Well, what kind of surprise?

HAL: I met someone—a woman named Marilyn. We're thinking about getting hitched. Anyway, we'd like Mark out here in California to live with us.

DWIGHT: Oh, well, he's got school, you know.

HAL: Well, it'd be after the school year was over. I'd drive out to Iowa and pick him up. This way he and Marilyn would have a chance to get acquainted. (Long pause.) Dwight? You there?

DWIGHT: Ah, that . . . that, uh, that won't do!

HAL: What do you mean, won't do?

DWIGHT: Well, uh, Mark's welfare means that he stays here with us.

The conversation ends when Dwight insists that Hal will just have to come out and talk to them about it. Having intentionally lied to Hal and confirmed his unyielding and uncompassionate nature, Dwight promptly hangs up without giving Hal a chance to reply.

When Hal arrives at the Bannisters, he is greeted by a cold and stubborn wall of resistance, symbolic of the grandparents' narrow and judgmental natures.

DWIGHT: Hal, I think it's probably time we talked about Mark's future. I want to adopt the boy.

HAL: What are you talking about?

DWIGHT (with righteous indignation): There's nothing personal about this. But you're irresponsible, Son, and you know it. . . . And it's for Mark's welfare that he be with his own family.

HAL (with conviction): "I'm his family. I'm his father."

DWIGHT (with judgment and finality): You send that boy poems he can't understand. And, God knows, neither can I. You're a romantic. . . . You'd be an interesting character for the boy to know. . . . You're not fit to parent him.

Hal returns to California, and in a later telephone call, Dwight again lies to him.

HAL: Hello, Dwight. This is Hal. May I speak to Mark?

DWIGHT: He's not here. . . .He's out camping in the Smokey Hills.

Hal asks when Mark will return and Dwight says he doesn't know. This conversation ends as did the earlier one—Dwight hangs up on Hal. We learn later that the "Smokey Hills" is the *backyard*.

At one point, in his frustration, Hal lashes out at all the stereotyped Christian characters Dwight Bannister represents with this emotional petition: "Lord, save us from the righteous people. That's all I know. God save us from the do-gooders of this world." The viewer is subtly led to interpret the selfish, unfeeling, and malicious Bannister as the symbol of righteousness.

When Hal finally consults an attorney, the attorney reminds him that Dwight Bannister is well thought of in the Iowa farm town where a court case would be heard. He reminds him that Bannister is on the school board and that he teaches Sunday School.

The courtroom drama itself clearly defines the hypocrisy, vengeance, and disregard for truth held by the Christian Bannisters. Hal's attorney questions Margaret on the witness stand:

ATTORNEY: Surely, Hal Painter must have some good qualities?

MARGARET (after a brief pause, crisply and shortly spoken): Yes!

ATTORNEY: Did you ever make an attempt to tell Mark what they were?

MARGARET: There was no occasion.

Margaret Bannister, throughout the movie, has been a model of cold and stone-faced self-control. She seldom openly reveals any deep thought or emotion and projects to the viewer a woman totally devoid of feeling. Finally, on the witness stand, she loses her "virtuous" restraint and in a brief, impulsive show of anger affirms that she indeed does *not* like Hal Painter.

Dwight, who has emphasized on the stand that he takes the boy to Sunday School, is unable to let well enough alone. Dismissed from the witness stand, he remains seated there and bursts into a bitter and angry tirade.

DWIGHT: I, uh, I don't see how anyone could like that man. He's worthless! Worthless for my son!

HAL: *Your* son.

DWIGHT (now out of control): He's a bohemian. . . . He writes strange poetry. . . ."

Eventually, Mark is allowed to live with his father. The movie's intention is clear. The viewer leaves with a warm feeling because the heroic humanist father is the winner. And the biased, cold, vengeful, and dishonest "Christian" grandfather—villain from the outset—is clearly the loser.

### Far from an Isolated Incident

Someone may think *I Love You, Mark* was an isolated incident. Quite the contrary, it is very typical. For instance, the CBS movie *Not in Front of the Children* followed the same pattern. "She's living with the man she loves. Now her ex-husband's revenge could cost her the children." So went the movie promo.

The movie centered on a mother who chooses to live with a man without benefit of marriage. Her ex-husband is represented as a Christian who attends church regularly where his father is the pastor.

The drama opens with tender, heartwarming music surrounding scenes of affection between mother, children, and mother's lover. One could almost shed a sentimental tear at the sheer beauty of the love between mother, lover, and children. Who in his right mind would question a relationship so wonderfully and tastefully portrayed?

Music stops. It is Sunday morning. Enter one obviously narrow-minded father who is upset at the thought of his children living under the same roof with their mother's boyfriend. Later that day, father and children attend church where the girls are bored by their grandfather's bland sermon. Sunday lunch is taken in the grandparents' home.

The preacher-grandfather, stern and forbidding, learns for the first time about the live-in arrangement. Following the reverend's tirade, one of the girls poses the tearful question, "Is Mommy going to hell?" A few days later, the ex-husband goes to his former home where the following conversation ensues.

EX-HUSBAND: Why didn't you tell me you were planning to have a man move in here?

EX-WIFE: I didn't think it was any of your business.

HUSBAND: You didn't think it was my business . . . if my daughters are living in an atmosphere of promiscuity?

WIFE: Living with one man doesn't constitute promiscuity . . . and besides, they are "our" daughters.

HUSBAND: Nancy, you are the person they respect most in the whole world, and you're teaching them that intimacy outside marriage is not a sin.

WIFE: I don't think it is.... One of the terms of our divorce is that they can go to church with you on Sundays.... They have the opportunity to hear your beliefs.

HUSBAND: But all the sermons in the world can't compete against what you're teaching them right here at home.

WIFE: I am being honest with them.... I am doing what's right for me, and later on they can do what's right for them.

HUSBAND: If you deliberately choose to have a relationship with some man, that's your right and your choice, even if I don't approve. But what about their rights? They didn't choose to live with this man.

WIFE: I asked them. They wanted to.

HUSBAND: They're babies! They don't know what it means. I forbid you to flaunt this relationship in front of my children." (Husband leaves.)

DAUGHTER (who has overheard conversation): Mom, are you gonna go to hell?

WIFE: No, Sweetheart, I'm not. This is kind of hard to explain.... Everyone has their own beliefs. And your daddy thinks the way we're living together is wrong. He has a right to think that. But I don't. I believe God is love, and that what we have together, Paul (her live-in lover) and I (beautiful, moving inspirational music starts again) and you two girls, that's love. And I think God understands that. That's what I believe. And when you two girls are all grown-up, then you have a right to decide what's right for you. OK?

DAUGHTER: OK. I knew God wouldn't send you to hell. (Music intensifies.)

Another crucial scene has the mother visiting her former father-in-law, the preacher. She challenges his narrow-minded orthodoxy: "What kind of love do you believe in," she asks, "the kind that makes a little girl believe her mommy is gonna go to hell?" Again she jabs the preacher: "Richard wants to settle out of court. He said he would drop this case in a second. But the poor man is afraid he's gonna go to hell!" The preacher, in a fit of anger, calls her a liar and promptly drops dead of a heart attack.

The remainder of the program is a study in contrasts. At one end of the spectrum is the harsh, bigoted, dogmatic, intolerant, domineering, ill-tempered, biased, overbearing Christian ex-husband. On the other side is the sympathetic, caring, kind, affectionate, gentle, understanding, tender, benevolent, secular live-in lover.

Throughout the program, the injured party is the teary-eyed ex-wife who is consistently a victim of Christian intolerance. In the end, the court finds in favor of the ex-husband, and only a last-ditch decision to get married to her lover keeps the children in the mother's house.

Everyone lives happily ever after—everyone, that is, except those whose chief defect is their Christian faith. The drama leaves the impression that they got what was coming to them. The clear teaching of the movie is that humanism is to be preferred over Christianity.

### Did Open Hostility Begin with the Movie M*A*S*H?

Perhaps this overtly hostile attitude toward Christianity began with the movie *M*A*S*H*. Obviously, when anyone dares to criticize the TV series "M*A*S*H," he risks reaction from loyal devotees who had a sort of religious dedication to the show. Perhaps some saw from the very beginning that the CBS series promoted a definitely humanist and subtly anti-Christian view of life.

If you look at the movie, which spawned the eleven-year TV series, you find nothing subtle about the anti-Christian bent of the production. It was vicious and unapologetic in its humanist orientation and its relentless attack on Christians and Christian values. Twentieth Century Fox produced the movie and Twentieth Century Fox Television produced the TV series. CBS picked up on the idea, and in 1972 the series was off and running.

In the movie *M*A*S*H*, now playing on television stations around the country, one of the principal figures, Major Frank Burns, is depicted as being Christian. The treatment of his character gives a perfect illustration of the anti-Christian stereotype so prevalent in entertainment today. The movie set the tone for Hollywood and network treatment of Christians for the movies and programs which followed.

In one scene in the movie, Major Burns, the Christian, enters the officers' tent and fires off a couple of pious judgments at hedonist Hawkeye Pierce. Then the Major kneels beside his bunk and begins praying aloud the Lord's Prayer. Hawkeye turns to Duke, who is equally amused at the behavior.

HAWKEYE: You ever catch this syndrome before, Babe?

DUKE: No, not with anyone beyond the age of eight years old, I haven't.

HAWKEYE (interrupting the prayer): Frank, were you on this religious kick at home, or did you crack up over here?

DUKE: Frank, how long does this show go on?

MAJOR BURNS (stopping his prayer): "It gets longer all the time. Now I have your soul to pray for and Captain Pierce's."

Hawkeye amuses himself and those outside the tent by singing loudly, "Onward Christian soldiers, marching as to war, with the cross of Jesus going on before." Outside the tent, a soldier takes up a rake in crosslike fashion, leading a group across the camp marching, laughing, and singing. Major Burns and his Christian faith are utterly embarrassed by the episode.

In another scene, Major Burns is teaching a Korean boy to read. When Hawkeye and Duke enter the tent, the boy is reading from the Bible. Duke takes out a pornographic magazine and hands it to the boy, suggesting that he will learn faster and profit more from its content. The boy rushes out to examine the material.

When next we see Major Burns, he is bungling through surgery, blaming his own incompetence on others. Every time a patient dies from resultant malpractice, Major Burns shrugs it off as the "will of God." Later Major Burns, who has a wife at home, goes to the tent of Margaret "Hot Lips" Houlihan. He explains to her that their sexual attraction for each other is the will of God: "It isn't just chance. I'm sure of it. God meant us to find each other." Margaret replies, "His will be done!" A scene of adultery follows. Major Burns, when last seen in the movie, is being hauled away from the camp in a straitjacket. He is obviously crazy.

But that is not where the mockery ends. The most riveting, graphic scene, which would be patently offensive to all Christians, occurred toward the end of the movie. Painless, the camp dentist, has decided he is homosexual and wants to kill himself. Hawkeye and others plan a deception to prevent Painless from committing suicide. One part of the plan includes a "last supper" for Painless. When the camera moves to the scene, thirteen men are seated at a long rectangular table, dressed in robes and striking poses exactly like those in the Last Supper painting by Da Vinci. No doubt is left as to the symbolism. Occupying the seat of Jesus is Painless and on either side are his profane and immoral friends in the seats of the disciples. One of his comrades even addresses Painless as "Rabbi." Hawkeye, conspicuous for his gutter-mouth and sexual escapades with various camp nurses, leads in the breaking of bread and passing of wine.

Painless is led to believe that a capsule he takes will be fatal. Friends pass by and place gifts in the casket which he can take into the next world—gifts which include liquor and pornographic magazines. The capsule-anesthetic takes hold and Painless falls asleep. Once Painless reaches a half-conscious state, Hawkeye convinces a nurse to have sex with him. As she enters the tent, Painless is laid out on a slab reminiscent of the burial of Jesus. Hawkeye has promised the woman that her sexual activity with Painless will bring the man back to life. The camera moves away from the woman as she is looking under the cover at Painless' genitals. Then the camera moves steadily upward as lighting and angelic music suggest an aura associated with resurrection.

What was it in the movie that appealed to CBS? Could it have been that the movie boldly, unapologetically attacked the very heart of Christianity—and that it fit well the humanist mindset of the network's media elite? For whatever reason, CBS chose to make a series out of a movie which front-to-back mocked, belittled, and scorned Christianity.

The humanist philosophy held by the TV writers and producers never appeared in the series with the savagery of that of the movie. What did appear was a subtle approach in which the only Christian was a witless, limited, incompetent, irrelevant priest. But maybe the subtle approach is more effective than the brazen.

As the years went by, however, the hostility became more open and honest. After "M*A*S*H" went off the air, CBS began airing a program called "AfterMASH." On one episode, one of the principal characters was Rev. Gentry, a religious "quack." Change the "e" in Gentry, and you have the name Gantry. Remember Elmer Gantry? Supervising producers of "AfterMASH" were Ken Levine and David Isaacs, who gave a big push for homosexuality on one of their "Cheers" programs. Levine and Isaacs would, I am sure, oppose any program which was anti-Semitic. All of us who care would. But Levine and Isaacs have no reservations concerning anti-Christian programs. In fact, they welcome the opportunity to produce them. In "AfterMASH," they effectively used Rev. Gentry as their stereotyped idea of a Christian—a rightwing, ignorant, fundamentalist, Bible-thumping, religious nut. Masquerading as humor, it was a vicious attack on Christians and Christianity. We first see Rev. Gentry as he walks up to a man outside the hospital and offers to help him get to heaven. Rev. Gentry says, "I spread the Lord's Word, free-lance, weekends mostly." Then he says, "Friend, is that despair I see in your eyes?" The confused visitor responds negatively. Unde-

terred, Rev. Gentry presses his case by telling the man that Satan
has him blinded by his afflictions. He then forces the man to his
knees and begins praying, "Dear God, help this poor soul." The
man interrupts Rev. Gentry and explains that he is not a patient,
only a visitor at the hospital. Rev. Gentry apologizes and offers him
a good deal on a used car from his auto dealership, "Enlightened
Motors."

The preacher collars another passerby and shouts, "Eternal life
can be yours." The old man replies, "My life is already eternal. I
spend half my time in the bathroom, which is where I'm headed
now." The old man turns to Colonel Potter, the hospital administra-
tor, and asks if he has ever seen a jackleg minister before. Colonel
Potter confronts the preacher and wants to know if he has received
clearance from the hospital to minister to the patients. Rev. Gentry
argues that the "Lord's messenger needs no clearance from the
hospital," and that the Lord has personally talked to him about the
spiritual condition of hospital patients.

When next we see Rev. Gentry, he is attempting to heal a young
man whose spinal cord has been severed. He tells the youth that the
people who are saying he can't walk are atheists, heathens, and
medical devils. He tells the boy that Jesus wants him to walk.

About this time, the chaplain comes in and orders Rev. Gentry
out of the hospital. The preacher calls him a "big city papist" and
says his problem is that he hasn't read his Bible. Otherwise he
contends that the priest would know that the same Lord who raised
Lazarus wants that boy to get up and walk.

The youth rises to his feet saying, "God wants me to walk, God
wants me to walk," and attempts to do so. But he falls on his face.
Father Mulcahy, the chaplain and the carryover from the movie and
television series, returns and counsels with the youth to find something that he can do well despite his disability.

So on the surface, one Christian is shown in a somewhat positive
light, while another is stereotyped as a religious charlatan. But even
the chaplain is the object of ridicule. Early in the program he is
shown preaching at chapel. Administrators and hospital personnel
are bored stiff with his sermon. When he suggests that he is close to
finishing, worshipers say "Amen." Colonel Potter turns to his wife
during the service and, with a frown, says that he hopes Father
Mulcahy is in the home stretch because "we've gone through the
Ten Commandments, the twelve Apostles, and the seven deadly
sins." Immediately following, Father Mulcahy says, "Consider the
Three Musketeers. . . ." The whole scene is supposed to be hilari-

ous. Clearly, the chaplain is shown to possess good qualities. But when he functions in matters which are inherently Christian, he is comical and irrelevant.

Not satisfied with just one anti-Christian program, Levine and Isaacs followed that program with another in a few weeks. Principal characters in the second program included a pair of angry, narrow-minded, rude, and obnoxious Christian parents who have a sick child in the hospital. The father is Baptist and the mother Catholic. Lesser characters include a self-righteous, bigoted Baptist preacher and a somewhat naive Catholic priest.

Father Mulcahy is escorting a mother to her child's room. They encounter the woman's husband, who has the Baptist preacher with him. An argument ensues between mother and father, priest and preacher.

HUSBAND: Mary! What are you doing with that fishstick?

WIFE: Father and I were just talking, Fred!

HUSBAND: He can rave about the Pope all he wants, but not to my kid. Rev. Horn here will give the good word to Jimmy—Baptist style (folds arms and assumes narrow, intolerant posture).

WIFE (shouting): Fred, you know how I feel about that!

FATHER MULCAHY: Now, now, now. We're all here to comfort Jimmy. And there's more than enough God to go around.

BAPTIST PREACHER: We've counseled mixed families before.

FATHER MULCAHY: Our two faiths have more in common than you might be aware of.

HUSBAND (pulling wife aside): You never give up, do you? Goin' around behind my back. Sneakin' fanatic! You people are all crazy. Burnin' candles and eatin' wafers.

WIFE: Yes, you Baptists make a lot of sense! Screamin' and dunkin' each other every week in that tank.

FATHER MULCAHY: Now, now, Mrs. Peterson. That dunking is their way of baptizing.

WIFE: It's ridiculous.

BAPTIST PREACHER: Mrs. Peterson, let's be fair-minded.

WIFE: Fair-minded? The Catholic way is the right way. Right, Father?

FATHER MULCAHY: Well . . . for us.

HUSBAND: Father, you're wrong! The Baptist church is the Word o' God. Right, Reverend?

BAPTIST PREACHER (smugly): Well, you don't see me arguing do you?

WIFE: Father, he's talking sacrilege!

FATHER MULCAHY: Well, I don't think the Reverend really meant it the way it sounded.

BAPTIST PREACHER: No, Francis. Actually I did mean it the way it sounded. That's why I said it the way I said it.

HUSBAND (haughty air, raised eyebrows): We Baptists are known for not beatin' around the bush.

FATHER MULCAHY: Well, they're certainly not known for their diplomacy. This just isn't worth being upset over.

BAPTIST PREACHER (talking to priest): You know, Francis, if I might say, with all due respect, one of the problems with you Catholics is you really do think you're above it all.

FATHER MULCAHY: You know, Ed, and with all the same "due respect," we're trying to work together. And you make a lot of remarks like that which are most counterproductive! (Father Mulcahy is now shouting.) In fact, all of them!

A fight breaks out among patients in the hospital who have taken sides with the two different factions.

## Prostitute Saves the Day

Then there was the CBS movie, *Dixie*. An angry member of the Catholic faith informed the Coalition for Better Television that the movie was anti-Catholic and decidedly anti-Christian. We checked it out. Here is what we found. The plot hinges on the sentencing of Dixie Cabot, who runs a house of prostitution in New Orleans, to a convent for ninety days—presumably for rehabilitation.

Before sentence is read, the judge asks Dixie the question: "Why do you keep doing this?" Dixie responds by saying, "I don't think what I am doing is wrong." Then she refers to serious crimes like stealing, rape, and homicide. "But", she says, "at my house, nobody gets hurt and nobody gets cheated." Now where have we heard that argument before? "Nobody gets hurt, so what's the harm?" That line of thinking fits perfectly into humanist categories. Everything is relative. There are no absolutes. Everyone ought to be free to do his or her "own thing."

Dixie is sent to the convent where she runs into trouble by paying a farm girl to secretly do her work. When reprimanded, she says, "Well, maybe I didn't play it by the rules, but I don't think I did anything wrong."

The convent falls on hard times and it looks as if it will close. The sisters are too stubborn to accept Dixie's worldly advice and foreclosure seems imminent. However, struck by pangs of conscience, Dixie sets out on a mission to save the convent. She rounds up two of her employees and sets out to blackmail the businessmen who are responsible for the economic woes of the nunnery. The mission is successful. Dixie returns to the convent for a hero's welcome. The sisters all run out with smiling faces to thank her for saving their home.

Another of the anti-Christian programs was an episode of ABC's "Hotel." In it, a priest is attempting to find himself. An unhappily married woman is hoping to find herself. They find each other. Within twenty-four hours, they find themselves in bed in the priest's hotel room.

Producers Bill La Mond and Joseph Wallenstein take great pains to make the illicit sex appear glamorous and desirable. As the priest and his lover reflect back on their night of passion, both agree that the experience was positive and enlightening.

Humanist teaching on sexuality was clearly evident throughout the program. Humanism, the religion of the leaders of the secular media, asserts that intolerant attitudes cultivated by Christianity unduly repress sexual conduct. Humanists believe that varieties of sexual exploration are not in themselves "evil," and that the rightness or wrongness of an act is dependent on whether the act is "fulfilling" to both partners. Viewed from the humanist perspective, adultery in this context was both right and desirable.

Those who believe in traditional Christian values view the action of the priest and the woman as immoral, wrong, and destructive. But from the tenor of the production, one would think that adultery was ethical, normal, and logical behavior.

As the program draws to a close, the priest justifies his feelings and actions by describing himself as, "Father Lawrence, holy man— Mr. Lawrence, just a man."

As the two lovers are about to part, Father Lawrence says, "You know, you showed me something about myself, Teri. It's a part of me that I don't think I can deny anymore."

Clearly, ABC wanted the viewer to know that the priest and the woman would be better persons because of the experience. Adultery was depicted as therapeutic for all concerned. The viewer was left with the impression that the priest would forsake the priesthood to pursue his newfound sexuality. Father Lawrence is congratulated by the hotel owner for his decision to leave the church. They are last shown headed to the bar to celebrate the decision. The viewer was also led to believe that the woman would return to her husband, a better wife for having made love to the priest.

Then there was ABC's edited version of the 1980 movie, *Resurrection*. It is an emotionally moving drama featuring Ellen Burstyn. Burstyn plays the role of Edna, a sensitive, compassionate, loving woman who loses her husband in a tragic automobile accident. She too is critically injured and "dies" for a few moments, during which time an otherworldly experience endows her with certain mystical healing powers.

Edna moves back to her rural farm home where she has every intention of living quietly for a few months in the aftermath of her husband's death. Things take a turn, however, when at a country picnic a little girl begins bleeding severely from the nose. No one can get the bleeding stopped. Edna gently takes the child in her arms and declares that the bleeding will soon cease. The bleeding stops and all are amazed at her powers. Soon after, she heals the preacher's son, who is dying of a stab wound.

Having also healed herself, Edna becomes aware that the powers are not just isolated occurrences. She finds that she can heal most people. Grandma suggests the gift is from God and she ought to use it for the common good. Edna says, "I don't guess I really know God. But if love is God, I guess I could try, Grandma."

Later, at a public meeting house, Edna heals a man who has been deaf for twenty-one years. An angry country preacher jumps up, waving a large black Bible. He is the epitome of narrow-mindedness, illiteracy, and religious bigotry. His face is red and distorted by alternate sneering and scowling.

PREACHER: I been watchin' these healins' of yourn' and you ain't never mentioned Scripture nor the Holy Ghost once. Now what is the source of this power?

EDNA: I don't know.

PREACHER: Oh, I think you do. (His veins are popping; his eyes are ablaze.) And maybe the reason you don't name it is because it comes from another place.

EDNA: And where might that be?

PREACHER: Hell itself, Edna Mae! (Preacher continues his tirade as Edna and others make their exits.)

Young Cal, the preacher's son, begins to move in on Edna. She stops with him for a drink at a local bar. Later Cal comes for a visit and he and Edna end up in bed together.

In another dramatic and beautiful scene, Edna heals a woman whose spine is hopelessly deteriorated. She is bedridden and unable even to sit erect. Edna lovingly embraces her and the healing powers flow. The woman rises to her feet and begins to walk. The congregation joyfully and tearfully celebrates the miraculous healing.

After attending several of the meetings, Cal becomes withdrawn. Edna notices that he isn't enjoying sex with her as much as before. Cal explains that he feels guilty because it just doesn't feel right having sex with a woman who is "holy." Edna responds, "Honey, if there is anything holy here, it's just the holiness of love, that's all. Believe me, I'm not the Holy Ghost. And I'm not exactly the Virgin Mary either. You oughta know that better than anybody."

Cal begins to search for the answer to Edna's power. He reads the Bible night after night. All those hours of exposure to the Bible prove disastrous for the young man. He goes berserk and charges wild-eyed into Edna's room, quoting Scripture. He says to her, "You are the living Christ. You are the Resurrection, the fulfillment of His promise to us." He tries to get Edna Mae to admit her messianic powers. She refuses and Cal leaves.

The next time we see Cal, he is quoting Scripture while he loads a shotgun. He intends to kill Edna. He finds her at an outdoor healing service. By this time, he is totally deranged, a madman. He fires the gun, wounding the healer. Cal is captured and Edna is taken for treatment. She quickly recovers and says good-bye to Grandma and the people she has come to love back home. Edna takes over a desert gas station where she quietly works her healing on passersby.

The last scene closes as Edna is affectionately hugging a pitiful looking, terminally ill little boy. She gives him a puppy and a healing embrace as the movie ends.

NBC's made-for-TV movie, *The Demon Murder Case,* had much to say about Christianity, none of which was positive. The plot revolved around a child who is "possessed" with many demons. Late at night a priest is called to help. He is irritated that the family should call at such an hour. He is cold and unfeeling toward the child, stating that he would rather be at home in bed. Several priests try vainly to exorcise the demons. They are shown to be powerless and fearful.

On the other hand, one young man is portrayed as caring and even asks the demons to leave the child and enter him. He calls on the name Jesus several times and implores the child to do likewise. We are left with the impression that he is a Christian. Later he moves in with a young lady without benefit of marriage.

## NBC's "Celebrity" Degrades Christians
The highly publicized NBC miniseries "Celebrity" portrayed "Christian" characters who were an affront to all those who in

sincerity profess the Christian faith.

The main character in the story is T.J. (Thomas Jeremiah Luther), one of the "three princes"—a name three boyhood friends gave themselves during their high school years in Fort Worth. The three get drunk in a deserted cabin the night before their high school graduation. While his two buddies watch, T.J. rapes a lost young girl looking for shelter. Thinking the girl dead, the three princes dump her body by a river and make a pact never to tell what happened.

The three take widely divergent roads to worldly success. T.J., the "prince of temptations," becomes a world-renowned Christian evangelist and faith healer. He is also a liar, a swindler, an extortionist, a rapist, and a murderer.

His name—Thomas Jeremiah Luther—is significantly symbolic, for it combines the names of a disciple, a prophet, and a leading minister of history.

But this Luther was created to disgrace and dishonor the revered names he bears. By sheer force of implication and by his actions, the character brings discredit on all of Christianity, especially on ministers of the Gospel. T.J. Luther is portrayed as a greedy, self-centered, despicable fraud. T.J. marries an heiress who introduces him to drugs, but he winds up burning their house when he is later unable to meet financial obligations to keep her in a sanitarium. He proceeds to become financially successful by operating a house of prostitution.

He eventually serves time for writing bad checks, but experiences a "religious conversion" just before his release from prison. He is immediately manipulated by Jonah Job, a small-time traveling evangelist who takes Luther on the circuit to give his testimony. But T.J. has dreams of his own and sets out to make them come true.

He calls himself "the Chosen." He is never ordained by any church. But he becomes wealthy and the idol of millions of people, many of whom appear to worship Luther himself. He builds a magnificent "City of Miracles" in Fort Worth, his hometown. His followers wear white robes and demonstrate their loyalty by their disruptive behavior in the courtroom when T.J. is ultimately tried for the murder of one of his princely boyhood friends.

Mack Crawford, the "prince of charms," becomes a football hero and ultimately a leading Hollywood actor. He is also homosexual. "Celebrity" portrays him in a sympathetic light, matched against his ex-wife and son. He returns to Fort Worth in a frantic effort to see his son, who has refused to talk to him for some ten years—ever since the boy (at about age ten) caught his father in bed with another man. It is Mack whom T.J. shoots to death during their "twenty-five-year reunion" at the same backwoods cabin of their youthful crime.

Adding to the anti-Christian tone of the drama was Mack's aunt, a deranged "Christian" woman who reared Mack. When he suffers a college football injury, she takes him from the hospital to "recover" at home. He grows worse until a friend discovers what is happening in the home—she has refused to let him get proper medical help. Later the religious fanatic aunt is shown attempting suicide during Mack's wedding to the physical therapist who helped him recover.

The third prince, Kleber Cantrell, is "prince of power." He becomes a highly successful journalist, writing for *Life* magazine. His return to Fort Worth is part of an effort to do a journalistic exposé on T.J. Kleber is injured by T.J.'s gunfire at the time Mack is killed. Only Kleber is ultimately absolved, as he decides he must tell all— about the rape and the hidden body twenty-five years earlier, and about the recent death of Mack.

In his murder trial, T.J. declares on the witness stand, "It was God Himself who pulled that trigger! God Almighty slew a devil!" Moments later, as Kleber reveals the twenty-five-year-old crime, T.J. meets a violent death, stabbed in the courtroom by the woman he had raped—a woman the three princes thought dead.

No one argues that such deranged fanatics have existed in the clerical ranks, but where is the balance? Most Christians are God-fearing, sincere, and dedicated; but to have the networks show Christians as such is apparently too much to expect.

### Humor at Christianity's Expense

The anti-Christian push is often promoted under the guise of comedy. The Bible, Christian theology, and the Presbyterian clergy were all objects of humor in the CBS movie, *Carbon Copy*. Very early in the production, Walter and his wife, Vivian, are shown in bed together. Walter is sexually stimulated but his wife is uninterested. A heated argument ensues.

VIVIAN: You have no right to force me, Walter.

WALTER: The Bible says, "Woe unto the wife who turneth her back on a horny spouse."

VIVIAN: The Bible doesn't say that, Walter.

WALTER: It did a long time ago. It was edited out by a lesbian translator.

When Walter's illegitimate black son comes for an unexpected visit, Vivian is crushed by the news. She responds by shouting,

"God will never forgive you for having a black child!" Walter counters by suggesting that God may be pleased, that maybe God is black. Vivian, shocked and outraged by the statement, screams, "You will burn in hell for saying that, Walter!"

Rev. Hayworth, the stern, insensitive Presbyterian minister is called to the troubled household. After praying with Vivian, Rev. Hayworth engages Walter in the following conversation.

REV. HAYWORTH: I don't see God's Book around, Walter.

WALTER: I'm sorry.

REV. HAYWORTH: Sorry is for those seeking forgiveness. Are you seeking forgiveness, Walter?

WALTER: Forgiveness for what, Reverend?

REV. HAYWORTH: Vivian said you told her that God is black.

WALTER: I simply posed it as a possibility.

REV. HAYWORTH: We don't speculate on God's color, Walter. If you ever want Vivian to speak to you again, go upstairs and tell her that God is white. . . . God is white. It's simple logic. His Son is white.

WALTER: That's not proof. I'm white. My son is black.

Rev. Hayworth sadly shakes his head and exits, saying, "I'll pray for you, Walter." Vivian decides to leave because she cannot forgive her husband for his earlier immorality with the black woman. The viewer is left with the impression that the poor simple-minded Reverend thinks the real issue in the family breakup is a domestic quarrel over the color of God.

"Saturday Night Live" is a forum for regularly ridiculing Christianity with the use of humor. One episode featured a mock-promotional for the NBC network. In referring to competition from other networks, the NBC announcer says, "You'd have to be crazy to watch it, or a godless Communist. Right, Reverend?" The camera switches to a preacher, sitting in his study thumbing through a large Bible. The preacher is identified as Rev. Luther Woodhead, chairman of Good Christians for Better Television. "Anyone," says Rev. Woodhead, "who watches 'Hotel' this year on ABC is condemning his soul to eternal damnation." The scene closes with the announcer saying, "NBC—watch it or die and go to h__!" Extended laughter followed.

That episode also featured Ethel, a Christian waitress whose favorite expression was "The Lord works in mysterious ways." At first, Ethel was told that her fiancé had married another woman. Then she was told that her house had been destroyed, her mother and brother killed, and that she had only one week to live. Each time,

Ethel responded, "That's all right. I should have expected it. The Lord works in mysterious ways." The sketch suggested that Christians are unintelligent parrots and their God is cruel.

## Writer Awarded for Anti-Christian Play

Not only is this anti-Christian attitude encouraged, it is even financially rewarded. Christopher Durang won the $25,000 Kenyon Festival Theater Award his play "Sister Mary Ignatius Explains It All for You."

Durang's play is a vicious anti-Catholic, anti-Christian presentation. Columnist Patrick Buchanan called it "perhaps the most anti-Catholic, anti-Christian piece of stage bigotry to be presented in the American theater."

Buchanan went on to say, "Fortunately, for Durang, his bigotry is anti-Catholicism. If he were as anti-Semitic as he is anti-Christian, he would neither be collecting awards nor staging many more plays." Buchanan was no doubt referring to the fact that Hollywood and the theater world is heavily influenced by Jewish people.

The theater world allows nothing anti-Semitic. (And that is as it should be.) But anti-Christian bigotry is financially rewarded. This is probably the result of the fact that there are very few Christians in the theater world. One gets the opinion Christians aren't allowed to gain positions of influence. The fact that the theater world would award Durang $25,000 for producing a vicious anti-Christian play seems to confirm that opinion.

A noted film manager agrees that the networks are biased against the beliefs and values of historic Christianity. Kenneth Curtis, general manager of Gateway Films, made the observation in an article which appeared in *NFD Journal*.

Curtis backed up his statement with facts on programs his company had offered to the networks. He said that even when films met all network requirements, but contained Christian values, the networks still refused them. Curtis cited the movie, *The Cross & The Switchblade,* which stars Eric Estrada from "Chips." He was told, off the record, that since the movie was based on the actual conversion experience of Nicky Cruz, that fact made it impossible to accept for telecast.

Curtis said the networks also turned down *The Hiding Place,* which has since been syndicated and is drawing 30 to 40 percent shares of the viewing audience where it is shown. "This film too has a strong Christian message, again based on historical events," Curtis said. "Interestingly, films made under the auspices of blatant alcoholics, adulterers, atheists, even a child molester or thief would be judged on the basis of quality, content, and commercial appeal. But anyone coming from a specifically religious orientation will not receive the same fair opportunity for consideration," he concluded. In my opinion, his comments are absolutely correct.

Even members of the secular media see this anti-Christian stereotyping. Clark Morphew wrote: "It has been so long since a television program gave a fair shake to men and women of the cloth that people are probably surprised when they go to church and discover a genuine human being in the pulpit." He cited as examples the Lutheran pastor on *Little House, A New Beginning.* "When his people ask him for help he becomes, at best, an uptight sacred presence and, at worst, a boorish nuisance. He is seldom a force for God and good," said Morphew.

Kevin Philips, a syndicated columnist for the Hearst newspapers, wrote: "The Coalition for Better Television is justified in charging that television news and dramatic shows tend to screen out Christianity and churches." Bill Reel, editorial writer for the New York *Daily News,* wrote concerning my calling attention to this discrimination: "I seldom agree with any idea out of Mississippi, but the reverend is absolutely right."

Neither are Christians exempt from this negative stereotyping by the network news departments. A segment of the "CBS Morning News," in which Morley Safer reported on the Wycliffe Bible Translators, makes the point.

Reporting on Wycliffe's work in Central America, Safer said that the aim of Wycliffe is to "resettle people into areas where they can be controlled and thus converted," building "instant slums" and "instant disillusion." According to Safer and the CBS report, Wycliffe people and other missionaries are doing harm.

What the viewing public did not know when Safer gave his supposedly "unbiased" report was that his wife, Jane, headed the U.S. division of Survival International, a London-based organization fighting Christian missionaries and missions.

In the spring of 1981, at about the same time Morley Safer and CBS were telling viewers that Wycliffe wanted to "control" people and offered "instant slums and instant disillusion," Jane Safer and her U.S. chapter of Survival International were holding a symposium in Manhattan that focused publicity on their objections to Christian missions.

Terry Drinkwater of CBS told a regional conference of a major denomination that religion is "hard to cover and underreported" on network television. Drinkwater said there were only nineteen religious stories on the "CBS Evening News" during 1982 and most of these were "here-he-comes, here-he-goes" stories about the foreign travels of Pope John Paul II.

## Networks Have the Last Word

Standard procedure is for Christianity to be censored from the news. But, if by chance, something distinctively Christian makes the news, a form of news manipulation comes into play. It can be quite effective. Let me show you how it works.

On the "CBS Morning News," Mrs. Myrtle Ricketson was relating a heartwarming human interest story. Mrs. Ricketson, an elderly woman, had not been able to walk for several years without aid of crutches. But when fire broke out in the room of her invalid grandson, she was able to throw down her crutches and quickly carry the boy to safety. At this point, Mrs. Ricketson said that she knew God had given her the strength. She mentioned that she had prayed and was sure that supernatural help had been given in her time of need. Then CBS newscaster Diane Sawyer broke in with these words: "It's amazing what adrenalin and love can accomplish."

Mrs. Ricketson gave credit to God. Diane Sawyer chalked it up to adrenalin and grandmotherly love. Sawyer's comment, in effect, corrected the mistaken ideas of Mrs. Ricketson.

I have been the subject of many biased articles. One, by Diane Holloway of the Cox News Service, appeared in papers across the country. Holloway had interviewed Tony Randall, who appeared as the homosexual character, Sidney Shorr, in the "Love, Sidney" series on NBC. In her article, Randall had a few choice words about me, calling me—among other things—a name I will not repeat in this book.

However, the interesting thing about the article was the fact that Holloway referred to a "barrage of attacks"—those are her very words—which I had aimed at the "Love, Sidney" program. I must admit that I was rather shocked, because I could not remember leveling any "barrage of attacks." I did, when it was announced that the lead character was to be a homosexual, raise the issue as to why it was necessary to identify the sexual preference of the character at all. I said that the only reason to do so was to present homosexuality as an acceptable, approved lifestyle. But, never mind. According to Holloway, I had leveled a "barrage of attacks."

The article brought to mind another incident, far more serious but very similar, mentioned by Franky Schaeffer in his book, *A Time for Anger.* When Dr. C. Everett Koop was being considered for the post of U.S. Surgeon General, the liberal media played the same game with him. I think it important for you to know that Dr. Koop was surgeon-in-chief at the Children's Hospital of Philadelphia, where the entire surgical center is named in his honor; that he is the inventor of many pediatric surgical techniques; that among the many awards for his medical practice was being made a member of the Legion of Honor by the French government; and that he is founder and editor-in-chief of the *Journal of Pediatric Surgery.* But did the major media play that angle? No. You see, Dr. Koop is also opposed to abortion.

In describing him, the *Washington Post* said he "was a leading anti-abortionist . . . a fundamentalist Christian . . . board member of two anti-abortion groups . . . and narrator of a controversial anti-abortion film." *Time* magazine referred to Dr. Koop as a doctor who had "made his name in the '70s separating Siamese twins." The *Boston Globe* listed him as a mere "clinician . . . with tunnel vision." NBC did a special on Dr. Koop and said that he was someone who "had appeared in a prolife propaganda film." NBC refused to list any of Dr. Koop's credentials.

Too often, those in the national media use their influence to slant and distort the news to their own perspective. A genuine concern becomes a "barrage of attacks" and a respected surgeon becomes only someone who "had appeared in a prolife propaganda film."

## Prejudiced Ears

The networks are sensitive to some groups, but not to Christians. The Black Anti-Defamation Coalition took offense at NBC's TV movie, *The Fantastic World of D.C. Collins.* In the movie, Gary Coleman plays a boy who fantasizes about movie and sports heroes—all of whom were white in the original script. Consequently, NBC altered the script to include basketball star Magic Johnson among the black child's heroes and eliminated Wyatt Earp and Tarzan.

The networks advocate selective viewing for those who find their programming offensive or indecent. Obviously, the networks practice selective listening. That is, they listen to some and ignore others. Voices of Christian people are ignored. Discrimination against blacks is an ugly thing, and the networks do not allow it. Equally ugly is the networks' discrimination against Christians, but on that issue the networks are happy to cooperate.

And tax dollars are used to help bring this anti-Christian theme to college campuses. A blatantly anti-Christian art exhibit at the University of Illinois at Chicago was vigorously defended as a work of art.

Some of the paintings by artist Douglas Van Dyke showed Mary, the mother of Jesus, seated on a toilet seat urinating on consecrated communion hosts; the Pope depicted as a devil or a jester; priests murdering people with axes; and a Crucifixion scene in which Christ has the head of a pig. The display was defended by James Overlock, director of campus auxiliary services. Said Overlock: "If we cannot show this, we are not a university."

This attitude is even carried over into decisions as to what books will be allowed on the "official" bestseller list compiled by the *New York Times* and other publications. That bestseller list is often anything but a bestseller list. For instance, in May 1982, the *New York Times* listed Jane Fonda's exercise and diet book as the number-one bestseller. It sold 17,500 copies during the month. During that same month, *A Christian Manifesto,* written by Dr. Francis A. Schaeffer, sold 35,000 copies, twice the number of Jane Fonda's book. Yet Schaeffer's book was nowhere on the list. One of the publishers of *A Christian Manifesto* cited this as a flagrant example of how those who hold the Judeo-Christian ethic are censored by our national media.

*Time* magazine and CBS, two leading members of the national media, each purchased full page ads in an edition of *Mother Jones* magazine to help pay for a vicious and sick anti-Christian article.

The article was a spoof of a movie concerning the life of Christ entitled "The Last Temptation." In the past six years I have seen many vicious anti-Christian skits and articles on television and in the print media. They have become increasingly more vicious. "The Raging Messiah" is the most vicious yet.

The article was written by Art Levine. If a Christian had written an anti-Semitic article half as vicious as Levine's article is anti-Christian, he would have been barred from nearly every print and broadcast medium in the country. That is as it should be. But Levine is supported generously in his anti-Christian writing.

A recent book published by Ballantine Books contains the following poem, set to music to the tune of "Stand Up, Stand Up for Jesus." The title of the book is *Not the Bible.*

O bloody bloody Jesus
I love your blood so red
I love the bloody corpuscles
Streaming from your head

O bloody bloody Jesus
I love thy crimson tide
I love the bloody Roman spear
That got stuck in your side

O rare and bloody Jesus
I love thy hands that bled
I love the nails that pierced them
O Jesus red and dead

I'd love to drink the blood O Lord
That drips from off thy feet
And wash my hands and brush my teeth—
O Lord would that be sweet!

O bloody bloody Jesus
I love thy blood so red
I loved you when you were alive
I love you better dead.

Ballantine Books is a division of Random House, Inc. The entire contents of *Not the Bible* are similar in nature to the poem. One of the book's authors, Sean Kelly, had this to say about it: "Anybody who is offended by it is probably someone I meant to offend." Kelly said of the Bible, which he said he read seven times in preparing to write *Not the Bible:* "It's a horrible thing." Kelly and his coauthor, Tony Hendra, didn't come up with the idea for the book or the poem. The idea came from an executive at Ballantine who approached Kelly and Hendra to do the book.

At an annual stockholders meeting of RCA, Reed Irvine of Accuracy in Media posed the following question to RCA chairman Thornton Bradshaw: "It has been pointed out ... that RCA is a significant advertiser in X-rated magazines ... magazines which are offensive to many—not only because of their exploitation of pornography, but because of their persistent ridicule of Christianity and Christian values. I presume that you would not advertise in magazines that are anti-Semitic or anti-black. Why do you advertise in publications that are anti-Christian? Is that less offensive than being anti-Semitic or anti-black?"

The comments were followed by a long pause. Bradshaw's response evaded the question. "I don't think this is fair for you to put questions like that. . . ."

DISCUSSION AND REFLECTION QUESTIONS
1. Why do you think those portrayed as Christians in the movie, *Mark, I Love You* were negatively stereotyped?
2. Have you seen a television program in which adultery was portrayed as being a sin?
3. Were you aware of the humanist orientation on the program "M*A*S*H"? (See chapter 1.)
4. Have you seen any television programs which were anti-Semitic or racist? Why do you think these programs aren't allowed?
5. The author has mentioned several programs which intentionally stereotyped Christians in a negative manner. Were you aware of this general thrust by the networks?
6. If Christopher Durang had produced a play which was anti-Semitic, racist, or anti-feminist, do you think he would have been awarded $25,000?
7. Do you think the media is fair, accurate, and unbiased in their reporting of matters pertaining to Christianity?
8. Why do you think the networks include so little about Christianity in their news?
9. Why do the networks listen to and react positively to the concerns of some groups, such as homosexuals, but not Christians?
10. Do you agree that Reed Irvine's question to Thornton Bradshaw was fair?

# SIX

# VIOLENCE TAKES A TOLL IN SUFFERING AND PAIN

What would you say is the nation's number one health problem? According to Dr. C. Everett Koop, the Surgeon General, *violence* is the nation's number-one health problem.

The Surgeon General said that the drastic increase of homicide and suicide rates could be related to violence on the tube: "The evidence strongly suggests that physicians ought to recognize that a diet of violent entertainment is unhealthy." Speaking to the American Academy of Pediatricians, Koop stated: "I think we physicians need to advise the patient (with problems of anger and violence) to get some professional counseling and also suggest that the parent monitor the entertainment menu and avoid the kinds of TV or motion picture fare that stimulates and contributes to the violence in their [children's] personalities."

Compared with all other advanced societies, the United States is by far the most violent country in the world. Our rape rate is many times higher than that of the United Kingdom. We have more homicides in Manhattan than all of England, Scotland, and Ireland combined. Our homicide rate is ten times that of the Scandinavian countries. Presently, *crimes of violence* are increasing at four to five times the rate of population growth.

This aggressive behavior is increasingly directed toward women and young girls. Since 1933, the increase in the rape rate in the United States is in excess of 700 percent. This means that the chances of a woman getting sexually assaulted are seven times greater now than then. That clearly indicates a change in male attitudes about sexual aggressiveness toward women. Why the change in male attitudes? Many studies indicate that in TV programming, sex is commonly linked with violence.

Dr. Victor Cline of the Department of Psychology, University of Utah, in summarizing the relationship between TV violence and violence in society, made these points: (1) we are the most violent advanced society in the world; (2) we have the highest rate of media violence (in our entertainment) of any nation; and (3) there are twenty years of behavioral studies linking exposure to media violence with violent behavior. Cline stated: "I do not think that any fair reviewer . . . can deny that the media are one important contributor to the violence problems in our society."

Cline went on to state that "repeated viewing also desensitizes the observer. . . . It becomes with repeated viewing more acceptable. . . . We lose the capacity to empathize with the victim. Man's inhumanity to man (or woman) becomes a spectator sport—we develop and cultivate an appetite for it, no different than in early Rome," he said.

What does research tell us about television violence? A research project of the University of Pennsylvania discovered the norm. In two separate studies by the group, children were asked, "How often is it all right to hit someone if you are mad at him?" The study showed that children who were heavy viewers of television, more often than light viewers, responded that it is "almost always all right" to hit someone. This and other studies have given parents justifiable cause for concern over the violent content of today's network television.

Violence in the real world is more often depressing than exciting. Not so in the symbolic world of television. There it is dramatic, thrilling, and entertaining. But underneath it all something subliminal is happening to viewers, both children and adults. It's called fear.

*The Morning Herald,* of Hagerstown, Maryland conducted a poll among its readers. The survey revealed that two thirds of those polled fear for their safety after dark—despite the fact that crime rates in Hagerstown are relatively low. The report further revealed that more than a third of the people felt they only had an even chance of escaping violent crime. Police statistics in Hagerstown show that their chances of being attacked are less than one in a hundred.

The paper also asked its readers about their television viewing habits. The results? Heavy TV viewers tended to overestimate all crime statistics about which they were asked to give opinions.

Studies show that heavy viewers of television are more likely than light viewers to answer questions about the real world in terms that reflect the world according to television. Heavy viewers are more inclined to be overly fearful of their own chances of becoming a victim of violence.

## Children Who Watch TV Heavily Are More Fearful

Children, particularly, are influenced. The Foundation for Child Development reported on a survey of 2,200 children, ages seven to eleven. They found that children who are heavy TV watchers were twice as likely as other children to get something. Can you guess what that something was? *Fear.* These children were twice as likely as others to report that they "get scared often." Violence is a shoddy way for networks to get a rating at a low price. But the price society pays for that violence is costly . . . very, very costly.

The National Coalition on Television Violence (NCTV) reported that aggressive behavior and an inclination to violence can best be predicted by two factors: first, children who are punished more harshly and rejected more often by their parents become more violent; second, the more violence a child watches on TV, the more violent adult he will become. These results came from the longest follow-up study ever done on human aggressive behavior. The researcher, Dr. Leonard Eron of the University of Illinois at Chicago followed more than 400 third-graders first studied in 1960.

Research by Dr. Paul J. Fink of Thomas Jefferson University in Philadelphia found that children and adults who watch prime-time TV are more prone to hostility and to seeing the world as a dangerous place. According to the NCTV, more than 2,000 studies confirm the relationship between viewing violence and real violence.

The networks have their unique way of dealing with these studies. In the summer of 1983, NBC released what it called a "new study" on TV violence. The study found no causal connection between television violence and aggressive behavior in children. The study involved interviews in "real life conditions" with 3,200 elementary school children and teenage boys. One of the study's authors cited poverty, aggressive neighborhoods, aggressive home environments, and drugs as causing more aggressive behavior than television. The study was conducted by NBC. Three of the researchers were NBC staffers. This "new study" was conducted from 1970 to 1973!

Let a child get a library card because the Fonz did it on "Happy Days" and the networks proclaim, "See how much good we do!" But let a thirteen-year-old boy sexually assault a four-year-old girl because of what he saw on TV and the same voices cry, "You can't hold *us* responsible!" In reporting the tension between TV executives and newspaper TV critics, *Advertising Age* says each group distrusts the other. Consequently, the networks try to avoid talking to the press. And the critics are fed up with contradictions that surface when the networks *do* talk. The article gave this example: "A network official will take great satisfaction in pointing out that an episode of 'Happy Days' in which the Fonz gets a library card apparently spurred thousands of children to do the same thing within days. But in almost the next breath, the same executives will say TV does *not* influence viewers' behavior. The stance is an effort to wriggle out of addressing questions on the impact that TV sex and violence have on viewers."

A CBS executive said that networks cannot allow the critics to influence them because there is little relation between positive critical acclaim and positive ratings. In other words, the networks assume no social responsibility for quality or content of their programs, except as they affect the ratings. In case you do not understand what that really means, it means that the networks are more concerned about their profits than about how their programs affect our children and our society.

Networks argue that people have always enjoyed being entertained by violence. They point to great literary works such as Shakespeare's *Hamlet* and Homer's *Iliad* as examples. They could also point to the Roman Colosseum, but for some reason they never do. Neither do they refer to their particular brand of violence like a network episode in which an ax-murderer chops off the head of a teenager and terrified teens are shown jumping over the bloody head lying on the dance floor.

The networks also argue that they act "responsibly" in the use of violence. On one episode of "Magnum, P.I.," Magnum had captured a criminal and could have taken him to the authorities. However, Magnum—the hero, the good guy—shoots the unarmed criminal, murders him in cold blood, while millions of youth and children watch.

## Networks Will Not Accept Responsibility

Networks have consistently refused to accept responsibility for crimes committed in imitation of graphic, gratuitous violence shown in their programs. Criminals imitate the violence they see. That's a proven fact. Alfred R. Schneider, vice-president of ABC, told a group of Florida college students that violence was very profitable for his network and that ABC had no intention of changing its practice. An article reporting on Schneider's speech said that the financial returns in airing violent shows are a factor in deciding how much violence is too much. "I work for a company that has to have a profit," Schneider stated.

The *NCTV News* tells the story of Brandon, a youngster expelled from school for violent habits he admittedly picked up from TV. He was not allowed to return to school until his parents restricted his television viewing. That was several years ago, and today Brandon is an adult who chose television as a career. He is Brandon Tartikoff, currently entertainment president for NBC, the very network whose study says there is no connection between TV violence and violence among children!

A letter, typical of the nonthinking, noncaring mentality, came across my desk. "If you don't like what is on television, turn it off." That seems like a good answer. If what is on the tube offends you, simply turn it off. But the answer was too simpleminded, too shallow. I wonder if the writer would also say that if I don't like crime in the street, I should then stay in my house. Or if I don't like drunken drivers on the highway, I should stay off the highway. Or if I don't like polluted water from the city well, to dig my own.

The "turn-it-off" attitude is very narcissistic, self-centered, and irresponsible. Whether I watch it or not, I have to live in the society which television influences. A few years ago, in a well-publicized incident, a mother and her young daughter were watching the movie, *Born Innocent* on NBC. When a scene came on in which a young girl was brutally raped with the handle of a plunger, she turned off the set. A few days later her little daughter was raped by a group of boys with a beer bottle who had seen the incident on the tube and had not turned it off. Turning it off didn't work then and turning it off does not work now.

Does TV violence affect us? Consider a typical letter which I received from a mother in Kentucky. "I would first like to say that I am a young (twenty-one) mother of two. My husband and I agree totally with you on TV. And it's filth. We now monitor everything our two-year-old daughter watches. We have had problems [she has nightmares] ever since she watched *The Exorcist* with us. We really didn't think about her being scared until we heard her crying and looked over and there she was with her hands over her eyes. That did it. Now it's 'Sesame Street' or something informing that we watch. What can I do to help? I have a son just a month old. What will television be like when he starts watching it?"

The Media Institute released the findings of a study concerning crime on television. Done by the research team of Drs. Linda and Robert Lichter of George Washington University, the study turned up some interesting information. The study found 1.7 crimes per show, more than two per hour. Murder was by far the most common crime on TV, with TV crime more than 100 times more likely to involve murder than real-life crime.

The Lichters stated that TV crime is twelve times more likely to involve violent crime than does real life. The typical motive for TV crime is greed and the typical murderer is a wealthy middle-aged businessman, a dramatic distortion of reality.

The study showed that all crimes are exaggerated on TV. Robbery is overrepresented sixteen times greater than reality. One area of crime that is vastly underrated, according to the Lichters, is that associated with alcohol, which the Lichters found twenty-five times more common in real life than on TV. (One must remember that the networks get millions of dollars in revenue from the beer and wine companies; therefore they are less likely to offend them with a true portrayal of alcohol's effects.)

The study showed that while violent crime is only 10 percent of real-life crime, it is 88 percent of TV crime. On TV, 76 percent of crime is committed by those over thirty. In real life, the vast majority of crimes are committed by those under thirty.

Police were much less successful in dealing with crime on TV than were private investigators. Private investigators were 100 percent succesful while private individuals were 97 percent successful.

The study brought to mind a quote by comedian Red Skelton concerning the networks. "They sell violence," Skelton said. "Now they say this doesn't affect your mind in any way whatsoever, but if you can subliminally sell a product in thirty seconds, what does one hour of filth or violence do to your brain?"

## Criminals Imitate TV Crimes

Frank Mankiewicz wrote a book called *Remote Control.* He said that he could not find a police chief in any major city in America who was not convinced that much of the crime with which he was dealing originated on television. He cited the example of Rod Serling who wrote a movie called *Doomsday Flight* in which a terrorist placed a bomb on an airplane which was set to go off if the plane dipped below a certain altitude. The skyjacker then broadcast his demands for ransom while the plane was in the air. While the movie was still in progress, a threat exactly like that on television was reported to police. Within the next few months, nine more similar threats were reported in major cities. Serling later said that he was sorry he had written *Doomsday Flight.*

In Bellevue, Kentucky a teenager copied murder scenes from the movie, *Helter Skelter.* The young man told police that he "just wanted to know what it felt like to kill" because his girlfriend had just left him. Consequently, he was charged with slashing to death a sixty-eight-year-old man and pouring acid over the body. He allegedly dragged the body into the apartment of his estranged girlfriend's sister. There he used lipstick to write "helter skelter" on the bathroom mirror. Then he used the victim's blood to write the same phrase on the bedroom mirror. A friend of the accused said they had watched the television movie *Helter Skelter* shortly before the murder. The movie tells the story of California mass murderer Charles Manson. When the movie first aired on network television, more than nine murders were traced to it. The movie was produced by Lee Rich, the same person who produces "Dallas."

Remember *The Executioner's Song* on NBC? It was the movie about Gary Gilmore. Following the program, twenty-year-old Jeffrey Alan Cox shot his seventy-seven-year-old grandfather four times in the head (similar to a scene on the program). He then turned on his seventy-two-year-old grandmother and shot her four times in the head. Both were killed instantly. Family members and law officials said they feel the movie triggered Cox to kill. He had no previous record.

In De Land, Florida a lawyer for a teenage youth said that fascination with characters in violent movies drove the boy to beat a seventy-three-year-old man to death. Jeffrey Leon Cypert, seventeen, was charged in the crime. The attorney said that Cypert was an "impressionable youth" whose identification with characters from movies such as *Friday the 13th, Prom Night, The Road Warriors,* and *Dawn of the Dead* caused him to overreact to alleged homosexual advances by the victim.

The total deaths directly related to the showing of *The Deerhunter* on television is more than thirty. The movie has been shown on several local stations and also on HBO, the cable network owned by Time, Inc. An additional thirty-one people have been reported as shooting themselves in the head while playing Russian roulette, graphically portrayed in the movie. If these deaths had been the result of a malfunction of a General Motors automobile, the car would have been recalled.

When police stopped twenty-one-year-old James Bazick in Wantage, New Jersey on suspicion of having stolen merchandise, they found a large club with spikes at the end. Bazick told police he got the idea for the club from the movie *Walking Tall,* which aired on television a few weeks earlier. Seventeen-year-old Cathy Ann Petruso of North Salem, New York hanged herself following an argument with her boyfriend. A few weeks later the boyfriend hanged himself. The couple had seen the movie *An Officer and a Gentleman* together several times. In the movie a man hangs himself at the end of his romance with a woman.

The movie *Texas Chainsaw Massacre* was shown to inmates at the prison in Chino, California. *Texas Chainsaw Massacre* is a violent, gore-laced movie about a family that turns its victims into barbecue. One of the inmates in the prison where the movie was shown was Kevin Cooper. Three days later, Cooper escaped. The following day, the bodies of Douglas and Peggy Ryen, their daughter, Jessica, ten, and neighbor, Christopher Hughes, also ten, were found hacked to death in the Ryen home a few miles from the prison. The gruesome hatchet murders of the four were a reenactment of the same type of violence depicted in *Texas Chainsaw Massacre.*

Topeka, Kansas police detectives in the juvenile division concluded a case in which a thirteen-year-old boy molested a four-year-old girl. One detective said the action was inspired by curiosity and not for sexual or violent reasons. The boy had seen several sex scenes on cable television and wanted to find out what sex was about, the detective said.

Jeffrey Gurga admitted stabbing to death Kathleen Pearson and wounding her daughter, Jeannine, after breaking into their Chicago apartment. Gurga, a former assistant state's attorney in Illinois, said he did not know either of the women, but was acting out fantasies based on violent scenes he studied on video-cassettes. He reportedly got the ultimate thrill in acting out bloody scenes he watched in movies which he recorded on video-cassettes. A lawyer in private practice, Gurga would walk the streets at night armed with a knife and fantasize about stabbing the women he encountered. Then he decided to act out what he had seen.

## Catholic Bishop Makes Valid Point
Catholic Bishop Mark J. Hurley of Santa Rosa, California made a valid point when he wrote the following: "TV network presidents and managers are wont to assert, in the face of contrary evidence, that no one has ever 'proved' one single criminal act as the direct result of TV programs. It may well be that such 'proof' is truly impossible because no researcher can really get inside the mind of a

human being," he said.

Driving home his point, Bishop Hurley stated: "Imagine a prospective sponsor for beer . . . being told by the TV advertising agency salesman: 'No one has ever proved that our advertisements for products has ever resulted in one single act of purchase.' Imagine the sponsor asking: 'If all the heavy emphasis on violence and sex has no effect on the viewers, what makes you think my ads will have any effect on sales?'

"TV is a powerful instrument for good or evil in our society," Bishop Hurley continued. It engenders values and promotes disvalues. To deny this power is blatant hypocrisy. No one in the world appreciates the real power of the TV instrument more than its managers. They hear the music of the cash register for themselves and their sponsors and measure success, so often, in those terms."

Bishop Hurley concluded: "They should not be allowed to carry water on both shoulders: When [John] Hinckley says he learned something on TV, it is dismissed as 'unproved'; when Coors beer employs dozens of athletes in its ads, it is affirmed as good business." Bishop Hurley is right on target.

What if you tie together pornography and violence? The more pornography men and women are exposed to, the less they consider rape a serious crime, according to one study. Eighty male and eighty female college undergraduates were randomly assigned to one of three groups. Over the six weeks of the study, a "massive exposure" group saw thirty-six porno films, each about eight minutes long; an "intermediate exposure" group saw eighteen porno and eighteen nonporno films, also lasting about eight minutes each; and a "no exposure" group saw thirty-six nonporno films of the same length. The researchers asked members of the various groups to suggest an appropriate prison term in the case of a local man who had been convicted of raping a hitchhiker but had not yet been sentenced. Men who had watched the nonporno films recommended sentences averaging ninety-four months, nearly twice as long as the sentence recommended by the men who watched the porno movies. Women who watched the porno films recommended sentences of seventy-seven months; women who did not watch the porno films recommended 143-month sentences. The results verify that the more we become desensitized to pornography, the less we consider rape to be wrong.

Another study done by researchers at the University of Wisconsin and UCLA confirmed that violent films spur some males to sexually assault females. The authors said their research showed conclusively that viewing violence—especially sexual assault—will motivate some male viewers to violent acts toward women. About 35 percent of the men surveyed indicated they would consider assaulting a woman if they knew they would not be caught, the study reported. The study indicates that television has desensitized viewers to violent behavior and reinforced myths that women enjoy being sexually assaulted and that some women "are asking for it."

Dr. Neal Malamuth of the University of Manitoba sent hundreds of students to movies. One group watched *Swept Away* (a movie about a violent male aggressor and a woman who learns to crave sexual sadism), and a second film called *Getaway*, about a woman who falls in love with the man who raped her in front of her husband, and how the two of them taunt the husband into committing suicide.

A second group of students were sent to see two control films, *A Man and a Woman* and *Hooper*, each containing scenes of tender romance and nonexplicit sex. Within a week of viewing the films, an attitude survey was administered to all students participating. Dr. Malamuth found that exposure to the films portraying violent sexuality *significantly increased male acceptance of violence against women.*

## Noted Professor Comments on These Findings

Commenting on the findings, Dr. Victor Cline of the University of Utah stated four effects of repeated viewing of violent sexual presentations: (1) they stimulate and arouse aggressive *and* sexual feelings, especially in males; (2) they show and instruct in detail *how* to do the acts; (3) the acts are in a sense legitimized by repeated exposure; and (4) there is increased likelihood the individual will act out what he has witnessed. Common sense has been saying the same thing for centuries.

Godfrey Ellis, professor of family relations at Oklahoma State University, says the sexually explicit shows on cable TV may be billed as adult entertainment, but children are frequently the viewers. He thinks children who watch adult programs may become sexually precocious or aggressive. In a sample study of 450 sixth-graders who watch cable, Ellis found 66 percent of the children watched at least one program a month that contained nudity, violence, or heavy sexual content.

Psychologists, medical doctors, and other professionals continue to document causes and to encourage methods to combat the rise in rapes. But the leaders in our society remain silent concerning the escalation of factors that contribute to rape. Among those factors are an increased spread of pornography and lenient treatment of offenders by the judicial system.

A Minnesota program to treat sex offenders requires rapists to swear off hard-core pornography, which one psychologist there describes as being "like a shot of whiskey to an alcoholic." Dr. Thomas Lickona, psychologist at the State University of New York in Cortland, points out that magazines like *Playboy* and *Penthouse* teach boys that women are sex objects to be packaged and marketed for the pleasure of men. Illinois criminal judge Christy Berkos gave a light sentence to a notorious plumber-rapist who, on top of prior rape convictions, pleaded guilty to five rape charges. Justifying the sentence, Judge Berkos said the defendent "had done things that did hurt the women, but fortunately he did not hurt the women physically by breaking their heads or other things we see. He didn't cut their breasts off, for instance." Connecticut psychologist Nicholas Groth says, "What we do in our society, whether it's in photography, films, or language, is devalue sex, and that gives the message that sex can become a weapon to degrade somebody."

It is a proven fact that when people become addicted to pornography, they become more likely to commit sex crimes. Consider these examples:

● *From New Jersey:* A young boy, exposed to pornography by a man, became so aroused that he brutally raped and murdered a ten-year-old girl.

● *From New York:* Girls, ages nine and twelve, told police a bookstore owner showed them pornography, then abused one of them. Thousands of pornographic publications were found in the shop when the man was arrested.

● *From Texas:* A fifteen-year-old boy viewed his father's collection of pornography, became sexually aroused, then dragged a nine-year-old girl into the bushes and molested her.

● *From Ohio:* A rapist confessed that he had been reading pornography prior to his assault of a woman on her way to church.

● *From Iowa:* A man was convicted of kidnapping and murdering an eight-year-old girl, and kidnapping and raping a ten-year-old. He confessed that one of the girls reminded him of young girl he had seen in a pornographic magazine and incited him to the sexual attack and, ultimately, the murder.

Stories similar to these can be repeated again and again. Police files are filled with such cases. Innocent people are victims of pornography. Still, otherwise respectable companies keep selling pornography because it brings in money.

## These Figures Represent Real People

We must remember that we are talking about real people, not just numbers and cases. A letter from a lady in a large Eastern city reminded me of this. "Dear Sir: I was watching you on the 'Donahue' show and I was very relieved to find out that someone feels the way I do. This is the first time I've ever heard about people that cared about what is on TV. A long time ago I was molested (I was only fifteen) and this person had *Playboy* and all kinds of porno. I guess . . . children's minds work different [ly], but mine told me that this might not have happened if he didn't have this stuff around. I've never told anyone this because it would hurt my family, so I wouldn't want it to get around. But for a long time people around me made me feel like I was just being silly for feeling so strongly about the rotten things on cable and TV. I can't tell you how relieved I am to know that I'm not the sick one. I'll help any way I can. Just tell me what to do."

Charles Keating, founder of Citizens for Decency through Law (CDL), gave some sobering testimony before the Senate Judiciary Committee. "Police vice squads report that 77 percent of child molesters of boys and 87 percent of child molesters of girls admitted trying out the sexual behavior modeled by pornography," Keating said. In one group of rapists, 57 percent indicated they had tried out the sexual behavior they had seen depicted by pornography. One of the many specific examples Keating offered was of seven Oklahoma teenage males who gang attacked a fifteen-year-old female from Texas, forcing her to commit unnatural acts. Four of the teenagers admitted being incited to commit the act by reading pornographic magazines and looking at lewd photographs.

A seven-year-old boy in St. Petersburg, Florida testified that he and his nine-year-old brother were imitating actions they had seen in their mother's pornographic magazines when they assaulted an eight-month-old girl who died in the attack.

The testimony stated that the sexual abuse of the infant, with objects the boys picked up in the bedroom, was mimicry of acts seen in porno magazines their mother kept around the house. The mother acknowledged she kept pornographic magazines and that the boys could have had access to them.

Tom McCoun, representing the nine-year-old, told the juvenile judge the younger boy testified that he and his brother, in sexually assaulting the infant with a pencil and coat hanger, were mimicking what they had seen in the magazines.

The infant was found on the floor in a bedroom where the two young boys were sleeping. She died shortly afterward. Medical examiner Joan Wood testified that the cause of death was "blunt trauma" to the chest and abdomen. She said it was consistent with one of the boys kneeling on the baby.

According to Robert L. Niklaus in *Religious Broadcasting Magazine*, pornography grossed an estimated $6 billion in 1981. According to police sources, in the Los Angeles area alone pornography made more money than Sears & Roebuck made nationwide. Besides the degeneration of morals, pornography gives another cause for great concern. The *Los Angeles Times* reported that some law enforcement officials estimate *organized crime* pockets about half of the $6 billion porn purse. According to Niklaus, that makes pornography the mob's third greatest money-maker, behind narcotics and gambling.

Joyce Kilbourne, speaking of the sexual stereotyping in advertising, referred to the fact that Brooke Shields was fifteen years old when she started advertising jeans. But more recent Jordache jeans ads feature girls nowhere near their teens wearing lipstick, eye makeup, and sexy hairstyles. Kilbourne said: "It's no simple coincidence that men's fantasies are turning to little girls. Now instead of ads that show us as helpless virginal creatures, we have ads with little girls as sex objects."

Child pornography has, in recent years, become a malignant cancer in the life of American society. According to Dr. Shirley O'Brien, University of Arizona human development specialist, child pornography flourishes, though it is illegal. O'Brien's findings are reported in a book aptly and simply titled, *Child Pornography*. Dr. O'Brien reports being shocked at the magnitude of the problem and says it is such a lucrative industry it will be difficult to stamp out. In her book, Dr. O'Brien considers child pornography anything that relies on sexual exploitation and abuse of children used as models or actors. Informed estimates of their numbers range up to 600,000 nationwide. That includes boys and girls as young as three years and as old as eighteen, but mostly ten- to sixteen-year-olds.

"These children are too young to know what they are getting into," she says. The harm done to the child, even if not physical, is real and long-lasting. That harm was the basis for a U.S. Supreme Court decision which upheld a New York State law against child pornography. The decision allows states to use a different free-speech standard for child pornography than they use for other material. Dr. O'Brien wrote me and pointed out that pornographic exploitation of children makes people react in one of five different ways: the first has never heard of it; the second says "live and let live" (they must be from the "can't-legislate-morality" school!); the third becomes sick, angry, and motivated to action; the fourth profiteers from it; and the fifth is sexually excited by it. To combat the tragic and senseless child pornography industry, O'Brien says the first and most important weapon is awareness. People cannot become involved in a cause about which they are not informed.

In their December 1983 edition, *Harper's Bazaar* presented an incredible, contemptible piece of "high class" child pornography called "Fabulous Christmas Fantasies: Tiny Treasures." Four full-page photos feature a beautiful little girl—perhaps six years old—openly exploited for the sake of feeding adult sexual fantasies. *Harper's* is a publication of the Hearst Corporation.

An Anderson, South Carolina supporter first alerted me to the tasteless article in *Harper's*, one of the country's most-read women's magazines. Describing her initial reaction, she writes, "Needless to say . . . I was very upset. All I did was tell my beautician about it and let it go at that. But from time to time I kept thinking about that little girl's face. The Lord has His way of reminding us of unfinished business."

*Harper's Bazaar* introduced a new, sophisticated attitude toward child sexploitation. The cherubic child stares mournfully from the four-page spread, her golden hair frizzed and piled high in adult styles, her sad eyes framed with adult makeup, her lips painted in garish hues of red, no hint of clothing in the chest-up photos. Her tiny fingers caress bottles of popular perfumes (Chanel No. 5, L'Air du Temps, Shalimar, and Estee Lauder), each sensually described in the accompanying copy.

*Harper's* writers chose such suggestive phrases as "the first feminine impulses that lead to a woman's delight" and "fragrances to express romance . . . seduction with just a hint of innocence."

The child's sorrowful expression suggests that even she is intuitively aware of the tragedy of her plight—used as a toy, a sex object, a plaything of adults willing to exploit whatever and whomever they must for their own personal gain.

Ann Wolbert Burgess, a researcher in the field, says that the public is becoming desensitized to the thought of youngsters as sex objects. Burgess is associate director of nursing research for the Boston Department of Health and Hospitals. In an address at the third annual Sexual Abuse Conference, she cited two examples of child pornography in advertising.

According to the Fort Worth, Texas *Star-Telegram*, Burgess told the conference that a recent issue of *Gentlemen's Quarterly* showed a nude six-year-old girl in a shirt advertisement. Burgess asked, "What is it about the ad that would sell a shirt?" *Gentlemen's Quarterly* is aimed primarily at the affluent professional man. It covers a wide range of subjects of interest to men but is not normally comparable to the men's pornographic magazines. It causes one to wonder exactly why the editors (and the advertiser) chose to exploit a nude child to sell shirts to men of upper social class.

Burgess gave a second example from *Vogue* magazine which reportedly carried an ad showing a six-year-old girl, heavily made up and nude from the waist up, advertising perfume. Both *Vogue* and *Gentlemen's Quarterly* are marketed by Conde Nast, a subsidiary of the Newhouse Corporation which also publishes *Parade* (the Sunday newspaper insert) and several daily newspapers in the United States.

A law enforcement task force on child pornography, child prostitution, and the kidnapping and selling of children has shown that the United States is the world's leader in using children for sexual exploitation and abuse. FBI agent James Murphy stated that children from three years old and up are being kidnapped for sex services and pornography. "You can order a child by height and weight," Murphy stated. According to the *CDL Reporter*, many of the children are murdered by the pornographers after they are finished with them so that they cannot testify.

## Strong Correlation between Pornography and Rape

What two things do the states of Alaska and Nevada have in common? Number one, they lead all other states in readership of pornography per capita. And, number two, they have higher rape rates than all other states. Alaska is number one and Nevada is number two in both categories. These facts appeared in a carefully researched study by Murray Strauss and Larry Baron, sociologists at the University of New Hampshire. The study also found, according to its authors, *"an unusually high correlation between sex magazine readership and the rape rate" in different states"* (italics mine).

Data for rape represented rapes known to and recorded by police, as given in the annual FBI Uniform Crime Reports. Magazines on which the study was based included *Chic, Club, Forum, Gallery, Genesis, Hustler, Oui,* and *Playboy.* Circulation was based on data received from the Audit Bureau of Circulation. With the exception of *Penthouse* (not included because it does not provide circulation data to the ABC), these are by far the most widely read sexually oriented magazines in the United States.

Though Strauss stopped short of saying conclusively that sex magazine readership causes rape, the raw data certainly tends to merit that conclusion.

Another recent study by John Court, published in his book, *Pornography: A Christian Critique,* found that countries which relaxed regulations on pornography experienced dramatic rises in the rape rate in the decade covering 1964 to 1974:

| | |
|---|---|
| United States | 139 percent |
| England and Wales | 94 percent |
| Australia | 160 percent |
| New Zealand | 107 percent |

The countries which continued restraint on the pornography industry showed a relatively small increase:

| | |
|---|---|
| Singapore | 69 percent |
| South Africa | 28 percent |

Japan, exercising a *more* restrictive policy, actually registered a 49 percent decrease in reported rape.

And if all this isn't enough, consider this. The Federal Bureau of Investigation data indicates that one of four twelve-year-old girls in the United States will be sexually assaulted during her lifetime.

## DISCUSSION AND REFLECTION QUESTIONS

1. The author says the rape rate has increased more than 700 percent since 1933. Why do you think this has happened?
2. The networks have never accepted the results of any study which showed a connection between violent programs and violence in real life. Why do you think this is the case?
3. Why are the networks quick to accept credit for instances such as children getting library cards after the Fonz did it on a program, but bitterly deny any negative influence from violence or immoral programs?
4. Is profit more important to the networks than the negative impact of their programs on society?
5. Will turning off the television solve the problem?
6. Do crime and violence on television accurately reflect real life?
7. Does television influence people to buy certain products? Does television influence people to accept certain values?
8. If General Motors produced a car which was found to have a defect responsible for the deaths of thirty-five people, would GM be forced to recall the car? If a movie was responsible for thirty-

five deaths, would the movie be recalled? Why?
9. Is child pornography an outgrowth of magazines such as *Playboy* and *Penthouse?*
10. Do you think the sales of pornographic magazines have anything to do with the rape rate?
11. Were you surprised to learn that one of four twelve-year-old girls will be sexually assaulted during her lifetime?

# SEVEN

# THE PUSH FOR HUMANIST VALUES

"Failure to rally around a set of values means that we are turning out highly skilled barbarians." No, the quote wasn't from a member of what the liberal media has tagged the religious right. They are, instead, the words of Dr. Steven Muller, president of Johns Hopkins University in Baltimore. Dr. Muller went on to say: "Society as a whole is turning out barbarians because of the discarding of the value system it was built on. . . . To restore its lost value system, America would have to return to its faith in God. There can be no value system where there is no supreme value that transcends man's natural self-centeredness, where one man's values are esteemed as good as another's."

Once, while I was debating Gene Mater, a vice-president of CBS, a question was posed by Marilyn Preston of the *Chicago Tribune*. When any question was directed toward me which had to do with values, I answered from my Christian perspective. Without apology, I admit that my value system comes from my Christian faith. I made no apologies for that during the debate, and I make no apologies for it now.

Preston asked Mater about *his* value system. Here's the way she put the question: "I'd like you to be as clear and as brave as Mr. Wildmon has been in stating his values. He obviously doesn't like a certain permissiveness and I'd like to know, what's the value system of television? Give us your own value system and explain how it relates to the problems of today."

Mater may have been a bit surprised by the question. "Well, I didn't know this was going to be a quiz about my own personal value system. I don't think I'm going to get into that. As far as the

CBS value system, I can tell you very simply that our belief is that television is there for two purposes. One is to inform, and the other is to entertain. In terms of entertainment, we try naturally to attract the largest possible audience for any given program. It's just that simple. . . . "

Mater continued without really answering the question. That's often the case in debates of this nature. Preston let him talk for a few moments, then she endeavored to get back to her major concern. Again, though, Mater's answer was elusive.

Finally, Preston interjected: "Mr. Mater, could you speak to the values? I understand the history of the swinging pendulum. . . . What I'm wondering is where is your network's pendulum now and would you speak to those values in as clear a way as Rev. Wildmon has?" How did Mater, the CBS vice-president, respond? Here is a direct quote: "Mr. Wildmon is a minister and has a stated set of values. I am a broadcaster and I don't."

There may not be a stated set of values, but the networks and Hollywood do promote values. What values dominate? Certainly not those of the Christian faith. CBS chairman, William S. Paley, founder and chairman of CBS for fifty-four years, stepped down at age eighty-one. David Halberstam in his book, *The Powers That Be,* paid tribute to Paley, whom he described as "perfectly suited" to his occupation. Halberstam said that Paley "was a sensualist and hedonist who was, at the same time, a rigorously disciplined and organized businessman." The man who guided CBS a "sensualist and a hedonist"? Indeed, television is guided by people at the networks and in Hollywood who have values which they teach very effectively.

Perhaps we can better understand the values which dominate the media if we examine their attitude toward pornography. What is Hollywood's attitude toward pornography? The *Hollywood Reporter,* the "bible" of film industry, issued a special adult film (pornography) issue. The magazine contained a section promoting the porno film industry, both movies and cable television. Nowhere in the entire publication was there a hint that there was a question of morality involved. In fact, the *Reporter* covered the issue in the same manner it would have covered a special Disney issue. In Hollywood, the issue is clear. A film is a film, and there is no moral difference between a pornographic film and a Disney film. They both make money, and that is the bottom line—morals excluded.

The attitude of the networks toward pornography is basically the same as that of Hollywood. The values endorsed and promoted by the networks were evident when ABC featured Hugh Hefner in an episode of "Laverne & Shirley."

The entire program was about the mad dash of beautiful young girls to fill vacancies among Hefner's Playboy "bunnies." In one scene, Hefner made an entrance to lengthy canned applause. He was treated as a guest of honor. One segment featured Hefner himself choosing the girl to fill the last vacancy. When another girl was chosen, Laverne was compensated in another way. She was to be Hefner's date for the evening which would include dinner and a romp with Hefner in the Jacuzzi, back at the mansion. The segment concluded with Hefner and Laverne leaving the bar arm-in-arm.

## Playboy Philosophy Shown in Very Positive Manner

Hugh Hefner and the Playboy "bunnies" were cast in the best possible light by ABC. Nowhere in the entire program was there a hint of opposition to the hedonist playboy philosophy—a philosophy which advocates free sex and recreational drugs; a philosophy which thrives on marketing young girls as sex objects; a philosophy which has no place for the poor, the physically unlovely, the sick, the elderly, the family.

There was a time when America's men would have been outraged by seeing their most beautiful young girls lured into showing their sexual organs to the public for money. There was a time when Hefner would have been considered a pimp instead of a celebrity. Many still consider him a pimp. But ABC doesn't. In our American homes, thanks to ABC, we've seen Hefner on TV singing, "Thank heaven for little girls, because they grow up in the most delightful way."

Here's a man who boasts of being raised in a Christian home, but now has overcome those early puritanical hang-ups. He has become an international corporate executive by showing moms and dads how to make a fortune out of their daughter's privacy. There was a time when anyone who attempted to get a teenage girl to pose for pornographic pictures would have been run out of town. But now, thanks to Hefner, when your daughter gets a job in most 7-Eleven convenience stores, it is a condition of employment for her to sell pornographic magazines over the counter.

The networks give Hugh Hefner an open forum for selling his hedonistic, humanist philosophy of drugs and sex to America's youth. That tells you something about their values.

All of this becomes badly confused with the real thing. Christie Hefner, Hugh's daughter, even had the audacity to refer to her father as a Christian. She said he was a Christian "in the truest sense of the word." Christie Hefner showed she was ignorant of either *Playboy* magazine or the New Testament when she made the statement. Knowledge of the contents of both publications would have prevented it. Miss Hefner is obviously ignorant of Holy Scripture.

Some supposedly religious organizations even honored this man whose philosophy is in sharp contrast to that of both the Old and New Testaments. When the Jewish organization B'nai B'rith honored Hefner as their man-of-the-year, it reflected the shallowness and sickness of those who made the decision, not the religion which gave us the Ten Commandments and, for most of us, our Lord Jesus Christ.

Not only do the networks endorse Hefner and his philosophy, they also help promote and legitimize his anti-Christian philosophy. NBC gave its approval to his sex-oriented magazine with a two-episode special of "Gimme A Break." In it the network made a joke of every argument against pornography. The program opened with Chief Kanisky sitting at the breakfast table. Neighbor Schwackhammer interrupts the meal when he brings over a pornographic magazine containing a nude picture of police officer, Mary Beth. The chief is outraged. Nell, the black housemother, and the chief's daughters see no cause for alarm.

CHIEF: D— it, the whole department is gonna suffer because of this.

SCHWACKHAMMER (the do-gooder): When police women start stripping naked, it's time for the public to go into action.

NELL: Yes, you should start a whole protest group. And call it Pinheads for Purity.

CHIEF (looking at centerfold in question): How could she pull such a cheap rotten trick? She's a disgrace to the uniform.

NELL: What uniform? All I see is a photograph of a very pretty girl. I mean, what's the problem?

CHIEF: A police officer should wear something besides a badge and a birthmark. (The chief's daughters enter, the oldest holding a copy of the pornographic magazine.)

DAUGHTER: Dad, have you seen this month's issue of *Joygirl* magazine?

DAD: How did you find out about this?

SECOND DAUGHTER: Barbara Wilson called this morning.

CHIEF: Her father lets her read this stuff?

SECOND DAUGHTER: Actually, it's her father's magazine.

FIRST DAUGHTER: Well, isn't it incredible about Mary Beth?

CHIEF: I don't want you girls looking at naked women.

SECOND DAUGHTER: Thank goodness. I'll never have to take another shower.

FIRST DAUGHTER: Dad, the centerfold of the month is a great honor. Dad, there's tremendous competition. And you really have to be something special. I mean, if I was asked, I'm not sure what I would say. (The second daughter begins examining contents of the pornographic magazine and Dad snatches it away.)

CHIEF: I suppose you think this is a great honor too, huh?

SECOND DAUGHTER: No. I think what she did was pretty stupid. I mean, all it does is encourage men to keep treating women as sex objects. On the other hand, I say if Mary Beth wants to let men exploit her body, that's her God-given right.

CHIEF: If God wanted women to run around naked, He would have made men nearsighted.

FIRST DAUGHTER: Come on, Julie, let's get outta here.

NELL: You know, Chief, you oughta give the girls a little credit. They *have* seen boobs before. . . .

As the chief warns family members not to "say another word" about the matter, his father comes downstairs with a copy of the magazine.

POP: Hey, Carl, have you seen this? Here's this lady cop built like Mount Rushmore. She says you were the first to appreciate her potentials.

CHIEF: Well, I wouldn't put it exactly that way, Pop, but. . . .

POP: There's only one thing I want to know. Has she got an older sister?

CHIEF: How could you look at that type of smut?

POP: I only look at it in the morning to get my heart started.

## Chief Told to "Keep an Open Mind"

The chief announces that he is going to have a word with Mary Beth. Just before he exits, Nell cautions: "Hey, Chief, when you do talk with the girl, try to have an open mind." Back at the precinct, the chief is greeted with the announcement that one of the squad cars has crashed into the river.

CHIEF: How the h— did that happen?

OFFICER: Oh, well, Sir, it seems that Benelli had left a picture on the seat of his patrol car, and while he was looking at it, he drove off a bridge.

CHIEF: Picture? What picture?

OFFICER: I don't know sir, but the last I heard, Benelli was still diving for it.

Mary Beth makes her entrance to the tune of several off-color remarks from other policemen. The chief calls her into his office.

CHIEF (holding up the nude photograph): Now just what is this?

MARY BETH: Take it easy, Chief. You got your finger on my belly button. . . . (The chief is not amused.)

CHIEF: *Joygirl!* How could you be in a magazine like this?

MARY BETH: Well, I tried *Field and Stream,* but they had a fold-out of a red snapper.

CHIEF: I want an explanation.

MARY BETH: OK. About two months ago a guy from *Joygirl* magazine called me and he said he had a snapshot of me, and would I like to pose for them? How he got my picture and phone number, I have no idea. I really needed the money.

CHIEF: Your mother was sick, and you needed the money for an operation?

MARY BETH: No, I needed the money for a down-payment on a new Porsche.

CHIEF: You mean that you posed naked for a sportscar?

MARY BETH: That's all they asked me to do.

CHIEF: Well, when people see a police officer naked in a magazine, how do you suppose they can respect the police department?

MARY BETH: Well, Chief, if they can respect a president who makes movies with monkeys, they can respect anybody.

CHIEF: What you did was wrong. It was stupid. And it was morally disgusting.

MARY BETH: Now wait a minute, Chief. That's not fair. I'm a good cop. In fact, I'm a d— sight better than a lotta the clowns you got working around here. Besides, what I do on my own time is my own business. That should be the end of it.

CHIEF: It is. Since you're so fond of taking off your clothes, turn in your uniform. You're fired.

MARY BETH: Fired?

CHIEF: You heard what I said. You're fired.

MARY BETH: You can't do that. Law enforcement's my life. It's all I know.

CHIEF: Good. Go get yourself a job as a security guard in a nudist camp.

MARY BETH: Listen. I have my rights, you know. I mean, you can't just fire someone over a difference of opinion. I'm gonna go to the civil review board. I'm gonna get my job back cause

I'm not gonna take this lying down.

CHIEF: Why not? It seems to be your favorite position.

MARY BETH: That's very funny, Chief. Let's see if the civil review board laughs when you fall flat on your face.

(Mary Beth exits to extended canned applause.)

The chief returns home to find that his whole family has turned against him in support of Mary Beth. His daughters refuse to speak to him or cook his meals. Even his father is out securing petitions for the rehiring of Mary Beth. The doorbell rings. The chief answers.

CHIEF: Pop?

POP: Oh, Kanisky, it's you. I thought you'd be out putting diapers on dogs. Now look here (speaking to Nell). We've got eighteen more signatures for Mary Beth.

NELL: That's good. Now, between you, me, Katie, and Julie (daughters), we've got over 200 names on the petition.

Chief Kanisky returns to headquarters where he finds a demonstration in progress. The pickets are well-dressed middle-aged and older ladies. Later, a small elderly woman who looks like everyone's grandmother charges into the precinct and begins hitting the chief with her purse. She too is angered over the chief's firing of Mary Beth.

The program, which was continued the following week, ends with a lunatic threatening to blow up the precinct with a bomb strapped to his body.

## "My Religion Is Getting Elected"

Immediately following the bomb scare, Chief Kanisky is summoned to the mayor's office. The mayor demands that Kanisky give back Mary Beth's job.

CHIEF: I can't do that, Your Honor. What she did was wrong.

MAYOR: You want to deal with right and wrong? Become a priest. My religion is getting elected.

The chief returns home and finds his family's attitude unchanged. He insists that he must stand for what he believes is right. The housemother, Nell, persuades him to give the issue more thought.

NELL: Chief, did it ever occur to you that there are two sides to this centerfold thing?

CHIEF: Two sides? You mean they photographed her rear end too?

NELL: I mean two sides to the issue. You know there are a lot of people out there that don't think Mary Beth did anything wrong.

DAUGHTER: I'm one of them.

CHIEF: Samantha, just for a minute, stop thinking about Mary Beth's rear end and start thinking about mine.

DAUGHTER: Do I have to?

NELL: Look, Chief, nobody likes to admit when they've made a mistake. Take me. When I accidentally burn the roast, do I tell you about it? No. I grind it up and pass it off as meatloaf.

CHIEF: Nell, I'm sworn to uphold the law. That's my job.

NELL: Chief, but you're also sworn to uphold the Constitution. And it says that you cannot deny a person a job on the basis of their race, religion, or how much clothing they have on.

CHIEF: What Constitution is that?

NELL: The same one that freed the slaves and gave women their rights and then forgot 'em both.

CHIEF: So if you had your way you'd have people going to work naked.

NELL: Sure would liven up the coffee break.

DAUGHTER: Yeah, and everyone would know everyone else's business.

CHIEF: You keep out of this. I did what I had to do.

SECOND DAUGHTER: What if you were wrong?

CHIEF: Look, somebody had to make a decision. And I had the courage to do it.

NELL: Even Mother Nature makes mistakes. That's why the elephant has to eat with his nose.

Chief Kanisky, having a change of heart, appears the next day at the press conference. His statement is short and sweet: "Three days ago I fired one of my police officers for what I believed was an inexcusable moral offense. I thought her actions were in poor taste and did a lot of harm to the dignity of the department. Well, maybe I was wrong. I'm not saying I *was* wrong. Just maybe. But in this country you don't convict someone on a maybe." Then, turning to Mary Beth, the chief says, "Mary Beth, I apologize and I welcome you back to the Glenlawn Police Department. . . . "

Mary Beth, smug and sneering, exits the conference. As the program ends, Mary Beth is congratulated and accepts a date with the policeman who had sent her picture to the pornographic publication. Hugh Hefner himself could not have made a better case for his anti-Christian magazine.

Even some businesses agree with the promotion of Hefner's values, rooted in hedonism and humanism. Anheuser-Busch sinks thousands of dollars into promoting the Playboy philosophy by sending a group of Playboy "playmates" across the country as goodwill ambassadors. These "playmates," whose claim to fame is that they have appeared nude in *Playboy* magazine, represent the company in retail account calls, trade shows and conventions, sports promotions, and other special events.

## Hefner, Man of Influence

The destructive nature of Hefner's philosophy, endorsed and promoted by the networks, hasn't escaped some in the secular press. *Chicago Tribune* columnist Bob Greene makes some startling and intriguing personal assessments in a article on Hefner. Greene credits him with being one of the two most influential Americans in the second half of the twentieth century.

Greene calls attention to the differences between America in 1950 and America today: a slackening of standards, an excessive freedom of expression, and a much less disciplined world. Hefner, through *Playboy* magazine and the message it proclaims, has changed America in ways we won't realize for generations to come, Greene said.

Because of Hefner we hear people casually using obscenities in public; we meet men and women who are openly living together outside marriage; we see young people getting high on whatever exotic substances they can obtain; we pass singles bars filled with men and women on the prowl for a one-night stand; we read in the newspaper daily of the soaring divorce rate caused by people bored and dissatisfied with the restrictions of married life; we see advertisements for X-rated movies or video-cassettes; we see people in T-shirts bearing suggestive or profane language; we are frequently upset by the aggressively selfish and self-indulgent attitudes we see in so many of our neighbors.

Quite an impressive list of credits! Greene continues, "Hugh Hefner let Americans know that they could behave in any way they pleased. Conventional ideas of morality didn't matter; the standards of one's parents didn't matter; the approval of one's peers didn't matter. All that mattered was that feeling good became an end in itself." The term for that lifestyle is "hedonism."

It is interesting that even the secular press has begun to detail precisely the decadent behaviors promoted by Hefner and those like him. With this general acknowledgement in the secular media of how Hefner-style philosophies relegate our moral climate to the gutter, one would expect a counterattack from somewhere.

You would think that the institutional churches would respond with such an outcry that pornography dealers would find themselves out of business. The ironic fact is that the institutional churches remain silent—surely not satisfied with the moral climate of our country, yet strangely silent.

In Hollywood this sexploitation, perfected by Hefner, is shooting for another market—youth and children. Ben Efraim, president of Unity Pictures, says he has found a proven method of producing a money-making movie aimed at the youth of America. His method appears to some as sheer exploitation. Efraim, producer of the cheap-shot *Private Lessons, Fast Times at Ridgemont High, Zapped!, Homework, The Last American Virgin,* and even *Blue Lagoon,* said the "important ingredients are comedy, sexual tease, and music." Efraim said that "voyeurism is an easily relatable comic situation and takes place in most of these films." He said, "My films may not be a high prestige product, but they are very lucrative." Some view his films as heavy on sexual exploitation and low on quality. Efraim has learned the art of exploiting our youth and is getting rich doing it.

One of his films, *Private School,* an R-rated release by Universal, was one of the most market-researched films ever. The target audience was boys and girls in the twelve-to-sixteen age bracket. In other words, children. Prior to release, two marketing problems surfaced. First, how could the previews be cleaned up enough to show on network television? *Private School* contained more nudity than nearly any R-rated film ever made. Second, Universal was concerned about the difficulty twelve-year-olds might have getting in to see the R-rated film.

Efraim was optimistic from the beginning that the children would somehow find a way. Quoted in the *Hollywood Reporter,* the producer said, "It is a very good target audience. . . . I really think I understand that audience and what it takes to get to them. . . . " In case you missed the point, the film was R-rated and the target audience Efraim and Universal were shooting for was the twelve- to sixteen-year-old group—children! The sexual exploitation of children is an accepted marketing technique in Hollywood. Even though twelve-to-sixteen-year-olds are not permitted in R-rated movies, Hollywood makes R-rated movies and then entices them to see them. One other thing. The nudity and the sexual exploits in the movie are provided by children. Adults making money by exploiting children—in Hollywood, that is good business. Next, they will be going after the eight- to ten-year-olds.

## Values Reflected in Program Titles
The values of the networks and Hollywood are reflected not only in the content of their programs, but also in the titles. The titles aren't

there by accident. According to *TV Guide*, the networks know what they are after. One executive of NBC said: "We look for words of movement, words of action. We like to have the word 'love' in the title if at all possible. If we can get an action word and 'love' in the same title, it's perfect," he said.

A CBS executive maintains that his network is "not quite as title-oriented as ABC or NBC, but admits that CBS is "looking for certain buzzwords that will get an audience's blood pumping. The best titles have the words 'Terror' or 'Diary of' or 'Portrait of.' You want to hint at sex but not make it too explicit," he said. He went on to say that those who title the films often have trouble with network censors, but, and these are his very words, "If you combine (sex) with violence, you're golden."

Paul Klein, former head of NBC programming and now with the Playboy Channel, says: "A title must have sex, love, but especially human abuse. Human abuse works far better than sex. Sex can scare off people over fifty. But roll it with abuse, and you get everyone. Klein showed something of the mentality of the networks when he went on the say, *"The very best title you could ever come up with would be 'Diary of a Rape'"* (italics mine).

Even Lucille Ball is disgusted with the situation. Concerning the TV scripts which come across her desk, the *Hollywood Reporter* quoted Lucy as saying that maybe one out of eighty is OK, no more than that." She added, "They're certainly not going for dignity these days. People don't care how dirty it is, just so long as it makes money." Lucy was asked if she would like to get back into acting. "Sure," she said, "I'd like to do a film, but I don't want to make a *Baby Jane* or a dirty one. I'd just like something good, and decent." Jack Paar, who hosted NBC's "Tonight Show" years ago, was interviewed by *Family Weekly* magazine concerning sex on TV and radio. His reply: "It offends me. I find it vulgar. I find some of the performers vulgar. It's such a tacky group of people today. I'm glad I'm out of it."

*Adweek* magazine described Ann Berk, NBC's new vice president of advertising, publicity, and programming, as a woman who can "juggle the demands of a career, a child, a lover, and a home with ease." Not too long ago we would have expected the sentence to read: "a career, a child, a *husband,* and a home."

An article by Joan Beck, columnist for the *Chicago Tribune*, pointed out some of the financial burdens and human hurts brought about by the promotion of sex as a commercial product. More than a million teenage girls a year are getting pregnant, most of them with unwanted babies. Four in ten teenage girls now get pregnant, and two in ten give birth. In 1978, the last year available for statistics, teenagers got 434,000 or 31 percent of all abortions. A total of 554,000 babies were born to teenage mothers in 1978, and more than half the mothers were not married. Eleven thousand of these mothers were younger than fifteen, and 203,000 were between fifteen and seventeen. The number of sexually active teenagers has gone up two thirds in the last decade.

Speaking about the government report on which her column was based, Beck wrote: "The report assumes teenage sexual activity will continue to increase. Maybe so, when it's actively implied or encouraged in popular music lyrics, in movies, on TV, and by about 30 percent of magazines on newsstands. . . . "

Remember that of the leading news media people, only 15 percent strongly agree that adultery is morally wrong, while of the entertainment elite—those responsible for our television programs—only 16 percent strongly agree that adultery is morally wrong. Also, 86 percent of the news media elite and 93 percent of the entertainment elite say they seldom or never attend church worship services.

## TV Gives Children New Heroes

Our children have not escaped the influence of this materialistic, hedonistic value system promoted by Hollywood and the networks. The *World Almanac* polled 2,000 eighth-graders in the United States to learn which persons they would like to be like when they grew up. The leading role models were, in order, actor Burt Reynolds, comedian Richard Pryor, actor Alan Alda, comedian Steve Martin, actor Robert Redford, and the late comedian John Belushi (who, as you remember, died of a drug overdose). Abraham Lincoln, George Washington, and other great figures of history were noticeably absent from the list. In fact, there was not a single name listed who was not an entertainer or a sports figure! How did those eighth-graders learn about their heroes? Through television, of course.

*Raising Good Children,* by Dr. Thomas Lickona, a developmental psychologist and professor of education at the State University of New York in Cortland, had a chapter entitled: "Television as a Moral Teacher—and What to Do about It." Lickona lists nine values our children learn from TV.

1. If you're having trouble getting what you want, try violence or crime. By age twelve, the average American child will have viewed about 100,000 violent episodes and seen 13,000 persons violently killed.

:e isn't anything to be upset about. Said one eleven-year-
I saw someone really get killed, it wouldn't be a big

wns are funny. That's the message of TV laugh tracks.
4. It's a rotten world. TV focuses almost exclusively on bad news; and the entertainment programs show businessmen, professionals, and law people planning or committing nearly half of TV crime.

5. Adults are dolts. When adults on family "comedy" shows are not depicted as dumb, they are probably shown as narrow-minded, racist, or self-centered.

6. Women are inferior. While blacks and other minorities have generally improved their TV image, women still are twice as likely as men to display incompetence.

7. Life is entertainment. As a result of thirty hours in front of the TV each week being passively entertained, a child is likely to think that gratification in life should come as easily as turning on the TV.

8. Drinking is where it's at. The highest rate of TV alcohol consumption occurs during prime-time and on the top ten shows.

9. Things make you happy. The average child sees 20,000 commercials a year. In those commercials and in the programs that sandwich them, we are constantly shown all the material things we should have and are led to believe that these things will make us happy.

Many young parents have voiced concern that "Sesame Street" may no longer be communicating the values they desire for their children. Some have questioned role models presented on the program which have included Richard Pryor, noted rock musicians, and others. One contributing factor may be Christopher Cerf, who now writes for "Sesame Street." Cerf is a former staff member of *The Lampoon*, a magazine majoring in irreverent, sometimes vulgar, and tasteless humor.

According to Dr. Domeena Renshaw, professor at Loyola University in Chicago, parents who think they are the prime influence in their children's lives are fooling themselves. Dr. Renshaw made the observation at a conference sponsored by the American Medical Association. She pointed out that children today are becoming sexually precocious because of overexposure to sexual materials. Such overexposure often leads to incest.

Remember the *Weekly Reader*? Still on the education scene, the publication recently revealed this discouraging result of a survey: One of every four fourth-graders says children their age feel "some" to "a lot" of pressure to try drugs or alcohol. One in four fourth-graders! Let that one sink in.

One day I received a call from a lady who began reading me some information supposedly regarding a child's toy. The name of the toy was "Masters of the Universe." From what she was reading, I assumed I was talking with a fanatic. So I told her to send me the material she was describing and I would do something about it. Little was I prepared for what arrived! What the lady had been telling me over the phone was absolutely correct!

### Children Told to Help Conquer Forces of Good

"Masters of the Universe" is designed for little children and comes with these instructions: "When you put on your skeletor helmet and armored belt, you become transformed into an agent of evil. Use your power sword and shield to combat good. With your mystical ram's head scepter you will be able to call forth the denizens of darkness to help conquer the forces of good." It was there! I read it. I still have it in my possession!

The toy was put out by Mattel, so I called Mattel. I was told by a vice-president of Mattel that the toy was produced without their knowledge, that they had received five letters concerning it, and that it had been withdrawn from the market. Two points here. First, the incredible thought that such a toy could ever go on the market and, next, that it would be withdrawn because five people cared enough to protest to the company! Can you imagine what the church could accomplish if it would dare lift its voice against the moral corruption which is affecting so many—children, youth, and adults alike?

Dr. Lois DeBakey, professor at Baylor College of Medicine in Houston, says the average doctor in this country earns $75,000 annually. Jack Klugman and Alan Alda, two of TV's celebrated actors who play doctors, earned more that that for one episode. Also, the two of them are among the hottest items on the lecture circuit to schools and even medical colleges. Author James Michener expressed alarm at the influence of TV and movies on youth. Michener says, "Young people are having their value systems formed by movies." He calls it an "underworld" of influence difficult to identify or assess. When I said that, leaders of the secular media called me a fundamentalist, rightwing censor, among other things.

Our youth have also been affected. A report by USA Today on college student attitudes revealed a disturbing change. It seems today's college folks are far more interested in making money than in personal development. The survey is an annual joint project of the American Council on Education and UCLA. They reported that 80 percent of the *1966* freshman class felt "developing a meaningful philosophy of life" was important. In 1982, only 45 percent felt that way. In 1966, 45 percent listed money as important. In 1982, 70 percent ranked it above personal values. "Saturday Night Live" is oriented to the youth of America. What kind of values does this program transmit under the guise of humor? NBC even considers child abuse a laughing matter. Take for instance a segment from one of the programs entitled, "Uncle Teddy's Little Theater." Uncle Teddy, a theater custodian comes on stage and announces that the play for today is "Grandpa's Watch."

"Grandpa's Watch" turns out to be a parody on child abuse. The scene opens with Mom and Dad and little Ricky sitting in the den. Mom announces to Ricky that she has destroyed the model ships he has worked on for six months. She has also killed his pet gerbils. Mom and Dad are upset with Ricky because he has made all A-minuses at school. His older brother is an all-A student.

Ricky says the problem is his eyes. He pleads for glasses because his head hurts and he can't see the blackboard. His father refuses and calls his son "worthless, spineless, stupid, and disobedient." He says to his wife that they should have drowned him in a sack when he was born. The parents leave and Grandpa enters.

Grandpa teases Ricky by offering him a gold watch and then taking it away. Later Grandpa hands Ricky a gun and recommends suicide as the only answer to the boy's problems. Ricky steals grandpa's watch and runs away from home. Audience laughter is heard throughout the program. Uncle Teddy closed the program by saying, "Join me tomorrow for a new play called, 'Debbie and Her Cigarette Burns.' "

NBC has a standard reply for those who object to the program's content. They say (and I'm using their own words) that "It is for people who enjoy innovative, contemporary satire." Only a deranged mind would place child abuse in the category of innovative, creative satire.

Brandon Tartikoff, president of NBC entertainment, hosted the 1983 season's premier of "Saturday Night Live." In his opening monologue, Tartikoff stated: "The reason I'm doing the show tonight is that I happen to be really proud of 'Saturday Night Live.' It's quality programming."

One week after Tartikoff's appearance, "Saturday Night Live" featured a segment called "Mr. Robinson's Neighborhood." The sketch was a take-off on the popular, wholesome children's program, "Mr. Rogers' Neighborhood."

"SNL" star Eddie Murphy ridiculed and vulgarized the Mr. Rogers character by first telling the boys and girls about his new friend, the landlord's wife. The language and innuendo left little for the imagination. Then he told the boys and girls about Juanita, a girl he last saw nine months ago. Opening a present sent from Juanita, the Mr. Rogers character finds a baby in a basket.

As the scene closed, he showed the boys and girls how to deal with the unwanted baby. He picked up the phone and called the local black market and agreed to sell the infant for $1,000. Laughter was well placed to tell us the activity was humorous. The Mr. Rogers character concluded the skit singing, "Tomorrow, tomorrow, I'll sell the brat tomorrow for a cool one grand. Good-bye, boys and girls."

"Saturday Night Live" has made fun of mental patients, child abuse, Christianity, physical handicaps, and even death and dying. But when a comic, representing a child's role model, makes fun of an infant sold in the black market, it's hard to imagine humor more diseased or depraved.

Michael O'Donaghue, contributor to "Saturday Night Live," was quoted as saying, "Humor is a release of tension, and you react to what is around you. The world is ready to nuke itself out. That's why my humor is preoccupied with death—Dick Van Dyke and Donna Reed just don't cut it anymore. I believe that life is a joke and death is the punch line," O'Donaghue said. Remember, "Saturday Night Live" is beamed at the youth of America.

Many young Americans are now choosing the ultimate escape from the chronic problems of living. An Associated Press report cited information from the National Institute for Mental Health that teenage suicide is a devastating public health problem in America today. Statistics show that 5,600 young people under the age of twenty-five took their lives in 1981. Suicides in that group rose 66 percent in the '70s. While television and the movies have told the teenagers to find the answer in sex and drugs, thousands of them are finding only death.

A survey conducted by the Connecticut Mutual Insurance Company found a vast difference between the values held by the news media, the general public, and the educational community. Sixty-five percent of the general public felt abortion was morally wrong, while among the members of the news media, only 35 percent felt abortion to be wrong. The educators disagreed with the general public even more—only 26 percent said abortion was wrong. Sixty-eight percent of the general public said pornographic movies were morally wrong. Among the news media, only 46 percent agreed. The educators were divided evenly, 50 percent saying they were wrong and 50 percent said they were not.

Among the general public, 47 percent said living with someone before marriage was morally wrong. Seventy-six percent of the news media said sex before marriage was not wrong and 70 percent of the educators agreed it wasn't wrong. In the area of homosexuality, 71 percent of the general public said active homosexuality was morally wrong. The news media found only 38 percent agreeing that homosexuality was wrong while only 30 percent of the educators considered it wrong. It appears that the leaders of the national news media and the national educational community have turned their backs on traditional Christian values. Remember that these two groups play a major role in setting values in our country.

The networks always tell us they are reflecting society, not attempting to influence or change it. Does today's secular mass media *reflect* the values of society or actively seek to *establish* their own values? The question was addressed by Dr. James Hitchcock, noted historian of the University of St. Louis. He said: "The mass media have the power to confer instant respectability. . . . No matter how seemingly 'neutral' the treatment, when certain ideas are given time and space in the media, they acquire a respectability that increases with frequency. Then comes the point where previously taboo subjects become familiar and acceptable." Hitchcock went on to add: "There is deep hypocrisy in the media's pious claims that they merely reflect reality and do not shape it. In fact, the power of celebrity is used deliberately and selectively in order to effect changes in values."

Dr. Hitchcock's perception was confirmed by an episode of ABC's "20/20," in which four couples are interviewed as representative of America's change in its thinking about the family. Tom Jarriel of ABC said in his introduction that the couples interviewed "reflect the way we are now, rather than yesteryear." Jarriel went on to state, "In the last twenty years, options of living together have changed—options not generally sanctioned in previous generations." Then "20/20" presented the episode on American couples.

### "Model Couples of Today"

Jarriel introduced the four couples. They included a lesbian couple; a homosexual couple; a heterosexual couple, formerly divorced, who lived together before marriage; and a couple living together, according to Jarriel, without the "restrictions" of marriage. Jarriel described the living-together couple as an arrangement "gaining in social acceptance."

Jarriel spoke in glowing terms about the homosexua Bruce and Geoffrey. Virginia Appuzzo, executive director National Gay Task Force, and her lesbian lover were describe typical lesbians who "place a greater value on spending tim together." Appuzzo was given time for a well-rehearsed defense of the merits of lesbianism. According to Tom Jarriel and the folks at ABC, "20/20" gave us important new insights into "the way we are now." My opinion is that ABC was more interested in promoting its own values than reflecting those of the American public

Hollywood and the networks say they don't want anyone, especially anyone Christian, imposing his values on society. But these same people work on a different standard when it comes to *their* values. NBC aired a program about some professional athletes who witnessed to their Christian faith in public places. NBC, which is owned by RCA, said, in effect, that those athletes should not be allowed to perform in schools because they witness to their Christian faith. But NBC/RCA finds it perfectly acceptable for other professional athletes to use NBC and the other networks to go into the homes of America to use their influence to tell teenagers and children that they should drink a certain kind of beer.

Lichter and Rothman said that their most astounding finding was that "two out of three (of those who are responsible for our programs) believe that TV entertainment should be a major force for social reform." Another of the findings by Lichter and Rothman was that only 16 percent of these people strongly felt that adultery was morally wrong.

We should not be too surprised to learn that 55 percent of all white teenage births and 83 percent of all black teenage births are illegitimate. The networks have been telling our children for years that sex outside marriage is the approved, socially acceptable norm. In fact, according to one government study, the networks tell our children that sex between unmarried people is five times more common than among married people.

This value of sexual immorality is strongly promoted in network programming, even in their children's programs. I call your attention to an episode of NBC's "Different Strokes," a favorite program with America's children. The series began as the heartwarming story of a wealthy businessman who adopted two poor black children. But then the program took a curious turn. Mr. Drummond, or Dad in the series, had generally been portrayed as having high standards

in one episode the producers of the
re they were headed and where they

set up for the children. However, Mr.
ded him to stay home for a couple of
o Dad sent the housekeeper on the
excuse was unexpected office work.
Dad brought home his friend, Miss
l. When rain cut short the camping
.....c only to find Dad sleeping with Miss
Saunders. Arnold, the youngest of the children and the friend of
every young child who views the program, couldn't understand what
was happening. So Dad explained his involvement with the woman
to Arnold. He explained that he was a man and Miss Saunders was a
woman, and that what he did was normal grown-up behavior. He
said that sex and marriage should not necessarily be related.

The program ended with Arnold proudly expressing his sexual
enlightenment. He says, "We understand; we're all adults here." The
message reached millions of impressionable young children. The
values were imposed. Those who say they don't want someone else
imposing his values on society did exactly what they say they oppose. There is a word for that. It is "hypocrisy."

The point is this: If you raise a voice of concern about the hedonistic and humanistic values being taught on television, you are out
of place. But it is perfectly all right for those who are responsible for
the programs to impose their values on you and your children.

Television is always teaching, forever communicating values. The
communication of those values comes through in cleverly devised
and contrived, emotionally moving programming.

Does Hollywood have a "father-confessor-motivator-director," a
"high priest" of values? The answer to that question is yes. His name
is Norman Fleishman, and, according to *California* magazine, he has
become the "key resource person for writers and producers seeking
information for shows dealing with any of his pet social issues,
including abortion, sexism, and the nuclear arms race." Fleishman
admits that his ultimate goal in dealing with those who are responsible for our television programs is to "get them to incorporate (his)
issues into their work. . . . "

### Does TV Reflect Society as We Are Told?
Does television reflect society? A poll by George Gallup shows it
absolutely does not. Gallup's poll shows that 87 percent of Ameri-

cans say that they have been influenced by Jesus Christ. Only 7 percent of the adults questioned said Jesus has had little or no impact on their lives, while the others had no opinion. A total of 90 percent considered themselves Christian. More than 75 percent say that Jesus is now alive and "lives in and cares for you," with 84 percent saying that "His Spirit is alive in the world." This is in sharp contrast with the leading Hollywood and network people who are responsible for our programs. Ninety-three percent of those people say they seldom or never attend church worship services.

And while Americans attend church, pray, and seek to take serious their Christian faith, network television gives a completely different view. Never is a modern-day Christian shown as a loving, caring, intelligent, compassionate person who contributes to society. Censorship, the thing the networks and Hollywood always cry about, could not be more complete against Christians.

The absence of Christians and Christian values is even more pronounced when another study is brought forth. The lack of a religious and spiritual foundation is the greatest threat to the American family today. This is the finding of a study by *Better Homes and Gardens* magazine. Some 200,000 people responded to the magazine's inquiry which looked at family life. Eighty percent of them saw trouble, specifying the need for a religious and spiritual foundation.

This loss of a spiritual family foundation is a far cry from what readers of the magazine said only a few years ago. In 1978, a similar survey showed that *inattentive parents* were the greatest threat to family life. In 1972, hardly more than a decade ago, the magazine's first such study on the family identified *materialism* as the primary threat to the family. Materialism, inattentive parents, and now lack of a religious foundation—sad facts of reality, one leading to the other in the breakdown of our country's most important institution, the family.

A totally unrelated source also puts the finger on loss of religious heritage as a cause of sexual abuse in our mixed-up society. Duke University alumni were told that Duke students today face drug-, alcohol-, and sex-related problems because the United Methodist institution has strayed from its religious heritage. Psychiatrist William P. Wilson, formerly with Duke Medical Center, made the statement at a reunion of the Duke class of 1943. Wilson asserted, "I know that many persons on the faculty and in the administration will say that a spiritual life doesn't make a difference, but they are wrong. They simply have not examined the evidence. . . ."

The psychiatrist bases his claims on his treatment of Duke students for several years, saying that the low level of religious emphasis shows up in the use of drugs and alcohol and related sexual mores which also lead to a higher incidence of abortions.

The first national study on the impact of religion on family stability concludes that the family with religious roots is less likely to experience divorce. According to *USA Today*, husbands and wives who consider themselves very religious and who attend church nearly every week are 42 percent more likely to be in their first marriage than those who never attend church worship services. Those with very strong commitment to their religious faith are 23 percent more likely to report "very happy" marriages than those who have no religious commitment. It really should not have required a study to tell us something that history has taught us all along. And it is a fact the media conveniently overlooks.

Earlier I mentioned the tremendous increase in suicide among our youth. Dr. Steven Stack, a sociologist at Penn State University, sees a relationship between declining church attendance and the increase in the suicide rate among young people. From 1954 to 1978, the suicide rate almost tripled for United States residents fifteen to twenty-four years of age. Stack noted that church attendance for the same age-group dropped from 48 percent in the 1950s to 28 percent in 1973. "Religion regulates individuals," Dr. Stack stated. "Apparently," he says, "if people have rules on moral codes to follow, they are less prone to suicide." That, however, is not the message of the media. The message of the media is for youth to free themselves from the influence of the church.

The Lichter-Rothman report confirmed the liberal social bent of the media and entertainment elite. Their attitudes have been implanted in Sweden. But a noted author says Americans had better think twice before adopting these standards. George Gilder, writing in *National Review*, had some sobering words of advice about the humanistic attitude toward the family and sexuality being pushed by the "family experts" and endorsed by network programming.

"The greatest triumph of expertise probably has been evinced in Sweden, where experts control family policy to a degree that could scarcely be imagined in the United States," Gilder wrote. "Every single goal of the left on family policy in the United States prevails in Sweden. They even have laws against spanking your children. They give paternity leave. They have every kind of antidiscrimination program; they have every kind of day-care support; they have every imaginable family-planning effort; they have sexual education from early childhood; they have really fulfilled entirely the mandate of the family planners," the noted author says.

## Do We Want Another Sweden?

But before we endorse the goals of the liberal experts on family-life and sexuality, Gilder says we had better take a long, hard look at the results. Sweden now has a 60 percent higher divorce rate than the United States. We have a terrible divorce rate, says Gilder; they have a divorce rate 60 percent higher. Half of all pregnancies in Sweden are ended by abortion, despite the fact that the Swedes have a wider distribution of contraceptive information and instruction than any other people. And despite the fact that half of all the pregnancies end in abortion, a third of all children born in Sweden are born out of wedlock. This is in a country that has fulfilled our agenda for enlightened family planning. "That's about three times the American rate of illegitimacy, which is itself depressingly high," Gilder stated.

Not all experts on the family come from Washington nor get their views concerning the family from network television programs. The closest thing to experts on family life I ever knew didn't come from Washington, and rarely are their values ever presented on network television. They wouldn't qualify for a position on the Planned Parenthood board nor on the advisory board to the networks. The most precious possession they ever passed on to their children was their Christian faith, and the experts would probably want the government to prohibit that. They were my parents. No program promoted by any so-called expert can ever take the place of the love of Christian parents.

Also in Sweden, the educational system is strictly controlled by the state. The official sex education program has explicit sex and contraception indoctrination beginning in kindergarten. Preteens are routinely *given* contraceptives. One recent publication reported that it is now suggested that similar "supplies" be given to children as young as seven.

It is amazing to me that Swedish officials are not alarmed at the negative results of the sexual permissiveness in their country. What are some of these results? From 1968 to 1974, venereal disease for girls under fourteen increased by 900 percent. From 1971 to 1975, legal abortions of all teenage pregnancies rose from 3.2 percent to 50 percent. In the 1970s, rape increased 400 percent. From 1960 to 1980, reported abortions in Sweden rose from 2,792 to 36,000. The nation's population is only eight million. Today, 92 percent of all pregnant girls fifteen or under have abortions. Over 85 percent of boys and 70 percent of girls have sexual relations before they are eighteen years old. The average girl's age at her first sexual experience is fourteen.

Besides these statistical data, there are other obvious factors accompanying this sexual permissiveness: open pornography; a widespread increase in venereal disease; divorce and the destruction of the family. The president of R.F.S.U., one of the agencies which collaborated on the sex education program for the schools, admitted that in his five years as president, the role and importance of marriage was *never even discussed.*

Where does all this lead us? It leads us to a cheapening of human life. You see, the humanist view of man is that he is only an accident and an animal. When you accept that view, natural consequences follow.

Among the consequences is abortion on demand. Abortion—not auto accidents, not heart attacks, not cancer, but *abortion*—is the number-one killer in America. Since 1973, when abortion was legalized, more than twelve million babies have been killed on abortion tables in this country. A pregnant girl or woman has the legal right to abort her unborn baby up to the time of birth. Among the civilized world, the United States is the only nation which permits fullterm abortion. The most unsafe place for a person to be today is in the womb; if a baby can escape the womb alive, he is legally protected by law.

There were over 2,769,000 American military personnel involved in the Vietnam War. Of this number, 58,655 were killed. There were 2,710,345 survivors. In the last decade, over twelve million unborn babies were involved in America's abortion war. There were no survivors.

Since the *Roe v. Wade* Supreme Court decision of 1973, those twelve million unborn children have been killed in a variety of ways which include dismemberment by suction, crushing extraction with forceps, and the burning away of the skin with salt solution. Since 1973, we have killed by abortion over twelve times as many *as were killed in the American Revolution, Civil War, World Wars I and II, the Korean War, and Vietnam combined!*

All of this is difficult to reconcile with the latest developments in the medical world. A recent study cited in *Encyclopedia Britannica,* 1983, contained a description of an amazing advance in medicine. Quoting from the article, "Prenatal medicine is now beginning to be able to intervene, before birth, to alleviate, and even cure conditions that previously would have severely compromised the fetus. This promises survival for thousands of threatened lives."

The same study contained this startling statement: "The concept that the fetus is a patient, an individual whose disorders are a proper subject for medical therapy *has been established* (italics mine). More than once in the study, the unborn were referred to in terms which included the following: *individual, patient, human,* and *life*—words conspicuously absent in pro-choice language popularized by the secular media.

It sounds much more humane to call it "pro-choice" than to call it "abortion." And it sounds far more acceptable to consider "termination of the fetus," than to think of "ending the life of a patient," "killing a human," or—"murdering a baby." *Time* magazine carried an article about the "pain" of abortion. Surprisingly, the "pain" to which the editors referred involved the guilt, fear, and anxiety of the *men* (referred to as "abortion veterans") who accompanied their wives, girlfriends, or lovers to abortion clinics. The article stated that "there is almost no one to help the million men who go through it each year."

While *Time* is busy gathering sympathy for the million "abortion veterans," it seems more fitting to gather sympathy for the tragedy and horror of twelve million "abortion victims"—the unborn innocent babies whose lives were casually snuffed out.

## New Values Leave "Imperfect" Babies to Die

In Bloomington, Indiana we saw a new twist to this casual disregard of human life. A newborn baby was discovered to have Down's syndrome. The baby needed serious but feasible surgery to enable food to reach its stomach. The parents of the baby refused to allow the surgery, choosing rather to starve the infant to death. The courts refused to order the surgery. Thus, with permission of the civil authorities, the innocent child was murdered by the parents and the state. The irony of the situation is that had the child been allowed to live, become a grown man, murder an innocent victim in cold blood, and then be sentenced to capital punishment, many organizations such as the American Civil Liberties Union (ACLU) and some church-affiliated groups would have clamored that his life be saved. But this innocent child, whose only crime was that he was born with a defect he could not help, had no such friends.

Just hours after the death of the innocent baby with Down's syndrome, "CBS Morning News" gave the lawyer of the parents a public platform to praise the "courage" of the parents in their decision to starve their baby to death. Thus we have taken another step in the process of determining that some of us, because of physical or mental conditions over which we have absolutely no control, are not fit to live.

Forty years ago this country was at war with a person we then considered a madman, Adolf Hitler, who was advocating precisely what our government sanctioned in Indiana. Hitler's policy of producing a superrace is now being practiced in our country. Now, for convenience sake, we take innocent life. The next step is taking the life of the elderly who are no longer productive and who use the resources that the younger, productive need. Don't say it cannot happen. It will happen if we fail to stop this hedonistic, materialistic, humanist value system which says human life is convenience, not sacred, and which is opposed to the Christian values we hold dear.

The day after the Supreme Court issued its latest ruling concerning abortion, two articles in most papers across the country stood in stark contrast. In one paper there were two headlines: "Court Eases Limits on Abortion" and "Sting Aimed at Eagle Killings." The first headline covered a story detailing the actions of the Supreme Court regarding abortion. Among other things, unborn babies older than three months may now have their lives snuffed out in abortion clinics rather than in hospitals, and parents do not have to consent if their daughters under age fifteen decide to take the lives of their unborn children.

The second article was on the crackdown and punishment of those persons who commit the atrocity of killing a bald eagle or even destroying the eggs. Isn't it odd that unborn babies do not have the weight of law to protect their lives, while unborn eagles do? The reason for this ironic twist? Could it be that we have turned from a society governed by a Christian view of man to one governed by a humanist view?

How do the networks handle abortion? They present it from their humanist view. NBC's "Buffalo Bill" was to "explore the delicate issue of abortion" on two episodes in early 1984, according to a TV columnist in *USA Today*. "We're dealing with life's issues on our show," said Jay Tarses, coexecutive producer. But to say that the show *honestly* "explored" or "dealt with" abortion is untrue.

What "Buffalo Bill" *did* do was make a mockery of the sacredness of human life. For example, coworkers of the single pregnant woman vote on whether or not Jo Jo should have an abortion. Jo Jo herself says simply, "I don't *want* this baby," and later, "I'm not gonna keep this baby."

116

What "Buffalo Bill" *did* do was hold the Christian faith up for ridicule. Jo Jo's boss, TV station manager Karl Shub, is the only character who makes any reference to a Christian belief. He is consistently a cowardly weakling who can carry on a conversation only by ducking his head, stuttering, and muttering unintelligibly half of what he says. Rarely can he complete a serious verbal exchange of more than one sentence. His ramblings just trail off into incoherent mumbling. He is never able to stand firmly for what he believes.

It is normal fare for the show to be irreverent. *USA Today* called it, "NBC's dark comedy about an ego-crazed Buffalo, New York talk-show host." Most would probably agree that he is far and away television's most egotistical, self-serving, and conceited character—a man obsessed with self and sex, using anyone and everyone for his own selfish gratification.

In the first abortion episode, Bill, arguing with his boss, screams, "If there's any rule I've ever lived by, it's that contracts are made to be broken!" Watching Bill in action for an hour or two would convince any viewer that that's exactly how he lives his life—all for self.

His adulterous relationship with Jo Jo White on the show has been quite open. When Jo Jo goes to Bill's office to tell him she is pregnant, the following conversation occurs:

JO JO: Bill, do me a favor; don't say anything for a few minutes. You know, you put nothing into this relationship, which is OK, 'cause I'm a big girl and I know all the risks. Lord knows, we all make a few sacrifices in order to have a warm body to curl up to now and again. But you lie to me, Bill! You tell me that I am important. You tell me that I am the only person you can open up to, the only one that means anything to you. You tell me a lot of things, Bill! And when I'm most vulnerable, I believe you. And I always, I *always* wind up feeling alone, dirty, and betrayed!

BILL: What is it, Baby, you want me to ask you out to dinner more often? (Laughter.)

JO JO: No!

BILL: Well, what is it? I mean I'm not a mind reader, I'm not gonna just sit here and take insult piled on top of insult!

JO JO (louder, growing more distraught): Bill, I get nothing back from you! When I am with you I feel like I am in a vacuum. You've never once asked about my plans, my dreams, my desires. I have them, you know! And what about my past? How did I get to this point in time? Who am I? Where did I come from? Does any of this matter to you?

BILL: I thought you were from Buffalo! (Laughter.)

JO JO: I am from Buffalo, d___!

BILL: Well, then what's your beef?

JO JO: My beef?

BILL: Yes! What is it? Why are you completely out of control?

JO JO: I'm pregnant.

BILL (drawing back, showing shock and horror): You're what?

JO JO: I'm pregnant—with child!

BILL: Well, you, uh, my throat's a little dry.

JO JO: You heard what I said, didn't you? (Bill nods yes in reply.) Now you don't have to say anything right now, Bill. But it would mean an awful lot to me if you didn't say something gauche and asinine. I mean it, Bill, think before you say what you're about to say!

BILL: Who's the lucky father? (Loud laughter.)

With a quick jab, Jo Jo knocks Bill backward across the sofa. Not content to let Jo Jo's hurt and frustration alone, the writers put a predictable insensitivity into Bill's next remark.

BILL: Gauche and asinine, right?

JO JO: I thought so!

A later scene in the same episode has Jo Jo going to Karl's office to ask for sick leave.

KARL: I hate to see anyone in pain, especially you.

JO JO: You think I'm in pain?

KARL: I know you're in pain.

JO JO: I am, Karl, I really am. (She breaks into sobs, then continues.) I feel so utterly stupid! (She and Karl both cry.) Would it be possible for me to take a few days sick leave?

KARL: Sure, but you know, I don't consider crying a sickness.

JO JO: What about pregnancy? What do you consider that?

KARL: I consider it a blessing. And so do most of the folks in my parish. But I think that, uh, I think you're not happy about. . . .

JO JO: Well, maybe if I were a member of your parish.

KARL: You're *not* happy?

JO JO: No, no, I'm not at all.

KARL: You mean being nauseous in the morning, stuff like that?

JO JO: I'm OK in the mornings. It's just the evenings I'm not crazy about.

KARL: I don't know why—I don't understand why you want to have a sick leave.

JO JO: I want a sick leave because I don't want this baby.

The episode ends with Jo Jo gone and another employee coming into Karl's office with a concern. Karl breaks down in tears to the sound of an extended laugh track.

The second abortion episode opens with Jo Jo telling her coworkers that she won't be in for a couple of days because she is scheduled for some minor surgery. It turns out that they all know about her pregnancy and have, in fact, voted on whether or not she should have an abortion. The scene is punctuated with frequent laughter.

Jo Jo demands, "How did everybody find out?" And Tony replies, "Heard from Karl." (So the Christian station manager in whom she confided betrayed her confidence.) Another coworker said he heard from Lenny, the retarded maintenance guy.

At the end of the scene, Jo Jo storms from the room in an outburst of anger and frustration: "I appreciate your concern, but I think I'm gonna leave it up to me, if you don't mind! Thanks for making me feel crummier than I already do!" As she leaves, she meets Karl and screams at him, "Remind me never to tell you anything in confidence!"

Karl, true to form, ducks his head, then meekly asks the group, "How did the meeting go?"

When Jo Jo meets Wendy, another coworker, in the hall, she tells Wendy of her pregnancy.

WENDY: What? Pregnant? Are you . . . ? Well, wait a minute, Jo Jo, you're not even married! (Laughter.) Oh, my G--! Well, wait, how did that happen? Well, I know how it happens. (Loud laughter.) But—holy Toledo! You know, nobody ever tells me anything around here!

JO JO: I'll tell you something. I'm not gonna keep this baby.

WENDY: I can understand that. You know, my mom got pregnant late in life. And her doctor advised her not to have the baby. She went ahead and had the baby anyway. Now, I don't wanta make you feel bad or anything, Jo Jo, but that baby was *me*.

Bill's assistant Woody arrives to implore Jo Jo to talk to Bill about abortion.

WOODY: I've been in communication with Mr. Bittinger [Bill].

JO JO (sarcastically): Oh, great! How is he bearing up?

WOODY: Well, he feels almost partially responsible for this dilemma. (Laughter.)

JO JO: Almost partially? (Laughter.)

WOODY: And, while on the one hand, he's delighted to know that he has active, healthy sperm . . .

WENDY (interrupting): It's not essential that I hear that—because I am, in many ways, still a child. . . .

WOODY: He feels, on the other hand, saddened that you're not more grateful. He hopes that you'll consult him before you do something rash.

JO JO: Why don't you tell him to go . . . (Laughter.)

WENDY: OK, you guys, I'm gonna go and mosey on over to the snack bar.

A later scene switches back to Bill, again illustrating his extreme vanity. He has moved back the furniture in his living room to play a child's fantasy game. Dressed in a New York Yankees' uniform, he prances about the room pretending to be a baseball star. In a one-man performance, he plays the roles of two announcers, the whole crowd—complete with cheers and boos, and himself as the hero:

ANNOUNCER #1: Now just a little human interest here. You know, Bittinger just found out the other day that he's gonna become a father. Well, that's just great, because as far as I'm concerned, there can't be too many Bittingers!

ANNOUNCER #2: Well, there's a little trouble in paradise though, Mel. Unfortunately, the mother has not quite decided whether she's gonna go through with that delivery or not. (Bill then makes crowd noises—boos and hisses, accompanied by an extended laugh track.) And I was just talking to Bittinger before the ball game. And he tells me that if anybody hits a ball over his head today, he's gonna have to permit the abortion.

As the senseless scene continues, Bill feigns making a great catch in the outfield. He falls over the "fence" (the back of his sofa) as one of the announcers yells: "I don't know whether he caught it or not, ladies and gentlemen. I just hope he's not hurt because that would be a terrible loss to the game. He caught the ball! I don't believe it! There will be no abortion! There will be no abortion! Listen to this crowd!"

Bill's insane, childish fantasy is interrupted by a knock at the door. It is Jo Jo. Bill invites her in.

BILL: Listen, it's all settled. You can have the baby. I know there was a lot of talk about you not going through with it, but I think it'd be a wonderful experience for you.

JO JO (clearly upset, not believing her ears): You do?

BILL: Absolutely. Honey, don't you understand you were born to be a mother? I mean, every time I think about it I get chill bumps all over.

JO JO (with obvious disgust): Really tickles you, huh?

Bill is so self-centered that he is incapable of realizing when others are turned off by his vanity. His conversation with Jo Jo continues.

BILL: Yeah. I mean, sure, I lost a lot of sleep over the whole thing, but I've reached a decision and I'm very happy with it.

JO JO: Really?

BILL: Yes.

JO JO: You want me to have this baby?

BILL: Absolutely!

JO JO: Then I guess that means you want to marry me? (There is no reply.) Well? (Bill looks down, finally nodding agreement. Laughter accompanies the scene.)

JO JO (lying): You don't have to marry me, Bill. 'Cause you're not the father.

BILL (astonished): I'm not the father?

JO JO: That's right! Think about it. Haven't we both been very busy lately, going our separate ways—me at the studio, you— (looking at his Yankees' uniform)—at the stadium? (Laughter.)

BILL: Then it was someone else. How could you do that to me?

Later, on the air of his "Buffalo Bill" show, Bittinger reveals the bitterness and vengeance which control his actions when someone has hurt him. He closes the show with this impromptu editorial: "I'm becoming a little alarmed about the amount of sexual promiscuity here in the greater Buffalo area. I'm not pointing a finger at anybody specifically, but I think it's about time you gals started taking responsibility for your actions. It takes two to tango. I'm not trying to ruffle anybody's religious feathers or step on anybody's toes. Be good to yourselves; be good to Buffalo; and start using those contraceptives or something a little more rhythmic." (Laughter.)

Following that editorial, Jo Jo reacts emotionally in the control room, revealing the disdain NBC holds for traditional Christian values. She explains to Wendy and Karl: "You know, I come from a nice, warm family—clean, sturdy, decent people. And they taught me how to be fair, considerate, respectable, and virtuous. And I've pretty much lived my life that way. I can honestly look back and say, 'Jo Jo, you turned out OK!' "

This comes from a woman who willingly goes to bed with the man who broke into her house to wait for her date to end, a woman who has described herself as "respectable and virtuous," a woman who is planning an abortion because "I don't want this baby." And she thinks she has turned out OK.

She continues her sad tale: "Now, here I am in the 1980s involved with a man who gives new meaning to the word "pig"—a man whose egomania has reached heights heretofore unimaginable, a man who publicly humiliates me in full view of the city where I grew up, where I still have family and friends. And yet, even though he embarrasses me, denigrates my character, belittles my morals, I still find myself drawn to him. Why? Because he never lets me down. I can count on Bill Bittinger to be absolutely awful. I can count on his despicability. Is that a word, Karl?

KARL (displaying his normal "Christian" character): Despicability, is, uh, acceptable, I think, in this context. (Laughter.)

JO JO: I think there's something really bizarre in me that attracts me to men like this. My ex-husband was semi-despicable. Did you ever meet him, Karl?

KARL (mumbling, apparently feeling the need to apologize): No. I, uh, I never did. I, uh, don't know why. (Laughter.)

JO JO: If you wanta go, Karl, why don't you go?

KARL: I, uh . . . (Karl turns to go. Laughter accompanies his exit.)

The closing scene has Jo Jo in Bill's dressing room.

JO JO: Bill, Wendy's waiting for me in the car. She's gonna take me to the hospital.

BILL: Well, I guess that's better than one of those bordertown roadhouses.

JO JO: I guess I'm in no position to tell you how absolutely horrible you were today for attacking me on the air.

BILL: What are you talking about? Did I name names? No. That was merely a gentle rap on the knuckles for you and a thousand wayward girls just like you.

JO JO (angrily): You're horrendous, Bill!

BILL: I'm hurtin', Jo Jo. You cut the slats out from under me. I was willing to let you have my child.

JO JO: How magnanimous of you!

BILL (growing angry): Don't use those multisyllable words on me, Baby! You're the one that was playing around. Now you're in trouble. Don't blame me for it!

JO JO: I'm leaving, Bill. I'll be in the hospital till Thursday.

BILL: Now you just wait a minute. Just wait a minute. Who was the guy anyway? I think you owe me at least that much!

JO JO: Oh, do I? Do you think wayward girls like me keep track?

The show ends with Bill softening enough to ask Jo Jo, "Is it gonna hurt?" Jo Jo replies, "I don't know," and leaves for her abortion. Another humanist sermon has just been preached.

The promotion of humanism has even had its effect on dictionary definitions. A Newark, Delaware resident recently wrote the following letter to a national religious publication:

"I looked up the word 'sin' in my old 1950 dictionary. It said: 'Breaking of law of God deliberately.' So I looked up the word 'God.' It said: 'The maker and ruler of the world. Supreme being.'

"I then remembered that I had a new dictionary copyrighted in 1979. 'Sin' was defined in it as 'The breaking of religious or moral law.' Reference to God omitted. I then looked up the word 'God.' God was defined as: '1. Any of various beings conceived as supernatural, immortal, and having power over people and nature, deity, esp. male one. 2. an idol 3. a thing or person deified or excessively honored.' "

Isn't it amazing how the meanings of the words "sin" and "God" have changed in the last thirty-five years?

## Humanism in the Public Schools
One issue which has been vastly discussed in the religious grassroots media, but to which the secular media—and indeed even the religious media—has failed to give much coverage is the issue of humanism in the public schools. An article which appeared in the January-February 1983 issue of *The Humanist,* magazine of the American Humanist Association, gives justification that those who say this is a serious issue have a valid point. Their point has been that those who identify themselves as humanists are, indeed, using the public schools to teach their godless religion. The article, entitled "A Religion for a New Age," was written by John Dunphy, a twenty-nine-year-old honor graduate of the University of Illinois.

Dunphy wrote: "The Bible is not merely another book, an outmoded and archaic book, or even an extremely influential book; it has been and remains an incredibly dangerous book. It and the various Christian churches which are parasitic upon it have been directly responsible for most of the wars, persecutions, and outrages which humankind has perpetrated upon itself over the past two thousand years." He continues: "I am convinced that the battle for humankind's future must be waged and won in the public classroom by teachers who correctly perceive their role as the proselytizers of a new faith: a religion of humanity that recognizes and respects the spark of what theologians call divinity in every human being."

Dunphy went on to say: "These teachers must embody the same

dedication as the most rabid fundamentalist preachers, for they will be ministers of another sort, utilizing a classroom instead of a pulpit to convey humanist values in whatever subject they teach, regardless of the educational level. . . . The classroom must and will become an arena of conflict between the old and the new—the rotting corpse of Christianity, together with all its adjacent evils and misery, and the new faith of humanism, resplendent in its promise of a world in which the never-realized Christian ideal of 'love thy neighbor' will finally be achieved."

Humanism has been ruled by the Supreme Court to be a religion. It is a religion which recognizes no god, has no absolute values, and teaches that man is an animal which came from nothing and will return to nothing.

Does the separation of church and state include the religion of humanism? Apparently not. It appears that those who have been saying that the public schools are being used to teach humanism have a valid point.

I found this bit of information from Christian educational crusader Mel Gabler's newsletter interesting. In 1940, the top offenses in public schools were as follows: (1) talking, (2) chewing gum, (3) making noise, (4) running in the halls, (5) getting out of turn in line, (6) wearing improper clothing, (7) not putting paper in wastebaskets. In 1982, things had changed: (1) rape, (2) robbery, (3) assault, (4) burglary, (5) arson, (6) bombings, (7) murder, (8) suicide, (9) absenteeism, (10) vandalism, (11) extortion, (12) drug abuse, (13) alcohol abuse, (14) gang warfare, (15) pregnancies, (16) abortions, (17) venereal disease.

Paul Harvey said: "I am opposed to putting garbage on television for the same reason I would oppose open sewers in our streets. It can be argued that what's in those sewers is 'natural' and 'normal' and 'everybody does it' and that it's 'not dirty.' But everywhere in the world where that sewage flows unconfined, it breeds disease."

Bing Crosby, in his last interview before his death, had this to say: "It became very apparent to me that very slowly and very subtly, writers and producers are working nudity, permissiveness, irresponsibility, profanity, scenes of semiexplicit sex, provocative dialogue, smutty innuendoes and situations into their shows. Moral responsiblity is almost indiscernible. . . . I voiced my sentiments to a TV executive and he said, 'We are only depicting life as it is.' I fear that they are depicting life as it is going to be if they are not diverted."

Paul Harvey and Bing Crosby were absolutely correct.

## DISCUSSION AND REFLECTION QUESTIONS

1. Do you agree with the statement that one man's values are as good as any other man's values?
2. What do you think is the value system undergirding the three networks?
3. Why do the networks present Hugh Hefner and his Playboy philosophy in a favorable manner?
4. Do you think that the networks use their entertainment programs to preach a social message?
5. Why do children select people such as Alan Alda, Richard Pryor, or Steve Martin as their heroes rather than George Washington, Abraham Lincoln, etc.?
6. What does it say about a society when it pays its teachers $15,000 to $20,000 a year and its TV stars $75,000 per episode?
7. Why are the values undergirding the media and those undergirding the general population often so different?
8. Why are the traditional family and traditional marriage so ignored by the networks?
9. Which do you think television does more often, reflect society or attempt to reshape society?
10. If twelve million children were killed in a war, the media would be outraged. Yet there is hardly any concern about twelve million unborn babies being murdered. Why?
11. Do you think the public schools often promote humanism in their classes? Why or why not?

EIGHT

# THE HUMANIST VIEW OF SEX IS NOT CHRISTIAN

Television is the greatest sex educator, or sex *mis*educator, in the country. Nowhere is television's anti-Christian, humanist theology more evident than in the area of sex. Sex, according to the networks and Hollywood, is basically an activity one indulges in whenever and wherever one desires. Close monitoring of how sex is handled on the networks easily confirms this. Monitoring done by the Coalition for Better Television of prime-time network television over a five-year period confirms that approximately 80 percent of all allusions to intercourse is between people not married to each other. After studying television carefully for seven years, I can recall no program on which the Christian view of sex was depicted as being either the norm or the approved.

Let me refer back to the Lichter-Rothman report. Only 16 percent of those who are responsible for what is on television strongly feel that adultery is morally wrong! The spring 1983 monitoring report of the Coalition for Better Television reported that of 651 implied intercourse scenes, only 147 were between married people. The other 504, or 78 percent, were outside marriage.

The people who control television incorporate their sermons on sex in their programs. A typical approach in preaching their humanist values about sex was the basis for a special two-part episode of "Amanda's" on ABC.

They have dated for three months. The time has come to get down to business. Zack is ready for sex. Amanda isn't. Good ol' Zack. Poor confused Amanda. Zack prevails. Amanda is liberated by the experience. Caterpillar turns to butterfly. So went the story-line.

Zack and Amanda are older adults who meet and become strongly

126

attracted to each other. The program begins with the two of them coming home from a romantic evening together. The following conversation ensues.

ZACK: I really do, really do, have something to talk to you about, and it's important. But I, well, I don't know how to begin.

AMANDA: You begin at the beginning. Come on, Honey, there's nothing we can't talk about openly and freely.

ZACK: It's about sex.

AMANDA: Bite your tongue.

ZACK: Bite my tongue? What's wrong with sex?

AMANDA: Nothing wrong with "that."

ZACK: You and I have been seeing each other for three months. And by now we know each other in every conceivable way.

AMANDA: Not *every* conceivable way.

ZACK: Exactly my point.

Zack persuades Amanda to come upstairs for a nightcap so they can pursue the conversation.

ZACK (proposing a toast): To the most marvelous, exciting, lovely woman I've ever met.

AMANDA: You haven't missed a trick. Brandy, moonlight, music. . . .

ZACK: You know, when two people love each other and want to be with each other all the time, it's only natural to be . . .

AMANDA: Romantic?

ZACK: Horny. (Extended canned laughter.)

Amanda attempts to divert the conversation, but Zack wants to know when she plans to have sex with him.

ZACK: Amanda, you know I want to sleep with you.

AMANDA: Yes.

ZACK: Do you want to sleep with me?

AMANDA: Yes.

ZACK: Then are we going to?

AMANDA: No.

ZACK: Why not?

Amanda explains that it has only been two years since her husband died, and that she can't help but think of him. An argument erupts and Amanda storms out.

## Amanda Apologizes, Gives In to Zack's Demands

Later Amanda comes back to Zack's room to apologize. Again Zack wants to know when he can look forward to sexual intimacy.

AMANDA: Oh my G_, is sex that important to you?

ZACK: Important? When you love someone, sex is the Fourth of July,

127

oman candles and pinwheels and skyrockets. Amanda,
ou ever feel the earth move?

in California you always feel the earth move.

up. Just tell me how many more years we're gonna sit
here together, drinking warm milk, and taking cold showers,
and watching the guest host on Johnny Carson.

AMANDA: Wait a minute, Zack. Are you, are you telling me that you'd
be willing to wait all that time and still stay with me?

ZACK: Yes d__ it, you are the most infuriating woman I've ever met.
I just said I love you.

AMANDA: O Zack. O Zack. The reason I didn't want to go to bed
with you is that I'm frightened. I've only been with one man
in my life, and these past two years with nobody, and I'm
scared. (Begins to weep.)

ZACK: Of what?

AMANDA: Of maybe not being able to please you. I mean, you've been
around, and I. . . .

ZACK: Thank you.

AMANDA: For what?

ZACK: For trusting me enough to tell me. That's all I really wanted.
And no matter what happens, I'll be pleased because I love
you.

AMANDA: Oh, and I love you.

ZACK: And I, I understand your feelings of fear. And if you don't
want to go to bed with me, I won't pressure you.

AMANDA: You mean you'd be willing to stay here with me even without the Fourth of July and the pinwheels and the rockets?

ZACK: Yes, but how about once a week a firecracker or two? (Canned
laughter.)

At this point, Amanda reconsiders and hops into bed with Zack.
The program ends when Amanda's son, Marty, accidentally catches
them in bed together.

The next week, the program began with Amanda attempting to
explain to her son the rationale for her actions.

AMANDA: Can't we talk about this?

MARTY: I can't talk to you about "that."

AMANDA: If it is so hard for you to use an uncomfortable word like
"that," then why don't we use another word for it?

MARTY: What other word?

AMANDA: I don't care as long as it's adult. How about "woo woo"?

MARTY: "Woo woo"? Naw, naw, Mom, it was a lot worse than "woo
woo."

AMANDA: Then why don't we call it "jire"?

MARTY: OK!

AMANDA: Honey, I know it was traumatic to burst in on your mother and see her "jire."

MARTY: Don't say that.

AMANDA: But it's a perfectly natural function, Marty. It's nothing to be ashamed of.

MARTY: Well, you never let me "jire" when I was a kid.

AMANDA: You weren't old enough to handle the emotional part of it.

MARTY: Well, obviously, I'm still not.

AMANDA: And there is another difference. I love Zack.

MARTY: Well, I never liked the guy.

AMANDA: Marty, what are you talking about? You told me you thought he was terrific.

MARTY: Well, he's not for you.

AMANDA: What do you mean, he's not for me?

MARTY: Oh, he's got you bamboozled so he can get what he wants. Mom, all I'm saying is don't give up real happiness for a couple of minutes of ecstasy. Don't be weak and throw away your most prized possession.

AMANDA: My most prized possession is my microwave oven. Marty, there is nothing wrong here. I love him!

MARTY: He is not gonna respect you in the morning.

AMANDA: Yes, he will. Maybe not as much as the night before, but. . . .

MARTY: Mom, if he really loved you, he'd be willing to wait for you.

AMANDA: Willing to wait? Marty, why do I get the idea that we have both died and come back to earth in different forms, with you as my father? Marty, don't you see what you're doing? You've never thought this way before. Suddenly, you're totally irrational. Why?

MARTY: Why? Because you're my mother. You shouldn't be carrying on this way. Especially at your. . . .

AMANDA: At what? At what? Say it. Say it.

MARTY: At your age.

AMANDA: Bingo! Now we are talking. Marty, I want you to tell me where it is written, in what hallowed pages, that sex is the exclusive property of the zits crowd?

MARTY: OK. I, I know what you're trying to say. But I don't know. To think of your mother that way. It's undignified. Mom, most older people I know don't even *want* to do it. Why can't you be normal?

dare you? You know something? I think it's time you
a little, my darling son, and realized that it's per-
rmal for people of all ages to have feelings and
And this happy, healthy, moral woman intends to sat-
isfy those needs up until her last moment on earth! And
maybe if I'm really lucky and God smiles on me, that will be
my last moment. (Amanda marches out of the room with
nose-in-air. (Canned applause affirms her statements.)

Later, when things have cooled down, Amanda again attempts to
talk with Marty.

AMANDA: You don't understand. You haven't a clue. Marty, think,
think. If the situation were reversed, and Dad were alive and
I were dead, which at the moment sounds appealing, if you
burst into that room and found your father in bed with another woman, you probably would have said, "Way to go
Dad!"

MARTY: Well, I might have thought that, but I wouldn't. . . .

AMANDA: Yeah, but would you have said, "Way to go Mom"?

MARTY: Well, of course not.

AMANDA: Why not?

MARTY: Well, because you never think of your mom. . . . Oh, boy, oh
dummy, dummy, dummy." (Marty is slapping himself on his
forehead.)

AMANDA: Let me, dummy, dummy, dummy.

MARTY: I'm sorry, Mom.

At this time Zack enters and says, "Oh, I don't mean to break up
anything." Amanda replies, "Oh, no, no, no. I think Marty and I
have finished our conversation." Marty gets up, but just before leaving, he turns and says, "Way to go, Mom." End of program. End of
sermon.

## Humanist Values Presented in Best Possible Light

The networks make good use of their made-for-TV-movies to incorporate the values they desire. ABC used its movie, *Intimate Agony*,
to continue the humanist sermons on sex. The leading character,
Dr. Kyle Richardson, takes a job on a resort island. He treats and
counsels several distraught herpes victims. Widespread ignorance of
the disease leads him to set up a herpes self-help clinic.

The movie gives valuable information concerning the physiological, psychological, and social impact of genital herpes, a disease
which affects over twenty million Americans. But was the movie
really about herpes?

Dr. Richardson, the leading character, is charming, clever, handsome, young, and sophisticated. If any person in the setting is worthy of emulation, he is. Other leading characters have glaring defects. But not Dr. Richardson. He is unselfish, caring, tender, loving, sympathetic—the perfect crusader and hero. He has all the answers. He is the teacher, and one by one his pupils come in for counsel.

Pupil number one is Katy, a teenager who contacted herpes from a boy with whom she had sex on the first date. Katy is surprised by Dr. Richardson's casual approach to her problem. "You make it sound like it's no big deal," she says. Dr. Richardson responds, "All the most dangerous things about herpes can be avoided." He goes on to state that related feelings are more dangerous than the disease.

Pupil number two is Tommy, the tennis pro. His life is shattered by the diagnosis of herpes, especially since the doctor insists he must tell girls about the disease prior to sexual encounters. Says Tommy, "You take away my boogie time and I'm nothing but a tennis shoe salesman with a tan." The doctor responds, "Nobody said you had to stop. You just got to tell."

Pupil number three is Marsha. She fears she has contacted herpes from a lawyer. Dr. Richardson explains that herpes is a "bug," a virus, and she has no cause for shame.

The only two characters in the program not having defective personalities are Richardson and his nurse. But eventually, both have statements to make in defense of free sex. Dr. Richardson makes his statement by going to bed with herpes-fearful Marsha.

At first, Richardson's nurse seems to possess the highest of morals. But she comes to the aid of the tennis pro who fears his "boogie" days are over. Quite unexpectedly she announces, to his utter delight, "I have nothing against making love to someone, once I care about them. If I get to know them well enough to care."

Admittedly, much of the physiological information concerning herpes is relevant to the lives of millions of Americans. But when you look at the psychological and sociological aspects of Dr. Richardson's counsel, it is the concept of sexuality which is promoted by humanism. In a nutshell, he teaches:

● That herpes is a "bug" and anyone contacting the virus has no cause for shame, regardless of the "how" of contact.

● Herpes should not limit the free expression of one's sexuality.

● That one having the disease can still enjoy a variety of sexual partners as long as one is careful to tell prior to sexual contact.

● And, by implication, that marital fidelity in itself is not an

wer to the problem, but rather, sex should be sched-
ninfectious stages.

## ...esome in This Family Program

...to have sex without emotional involvement was the theme of
one episode of RCA/NBC's "Family Ties." A concerned father in
Moline, Illinois sent me a copy of a letter he had written to NBC's
Albert Kroeger concerning the program.

"Dear Mr. Kroeger: On Wednesday evening, August 31, 1983, my
family settled down to watch some television together. As is often
the case, we turned on the local NBC station, WOC-TV in Davenport,
Iowa to watch a family-oriented, situation comedy, 'Family Ties.' I
was shocked and my children embarrassed when the seventeen-year-
old boy in the program was suddenly seduced to bed by a college
girl. . . . "

The father went on to state, "Our moral sensibilities were further
shocked when the father in the program learned of his son's sexual
escapade: he joked about it, and showed his approval by offering
counsel so 'next time' the son would not be emotionally entangled
in such casual sex."

A thorough review of the program revealed that the father from
Moline had not exaggerated his comments. This particular episode,
created and produced by David Goldberg, was a lesson on how to
have sex without love or commitment and especially without marriage. Early in the program, Alex, the seventeen-year-old, comes
home from his "night out" with an "older woman," describing it as
a tremendously maturing experience. Mother's only objection is that
he should have called home so she would not worry.

Very quickly, young Alex learns that he has taken the sexual
encounter more seriously than Stephanie, the woman involved. Alex
decides that he ought to give up on women and join a monastery.
Dad counsels the son on crucial points.

Number one: He offers acceptance and affirmation of his son's
first sex experience. It is a great day in the boy's life. Number two:
Dad cautions his son to learn to separate sex from love. He suggests
that sexual involvement should not necessarily be connected to love
and commitment. At one point, Dad states: "Alex, you and Stephanie may have had a beautiful night together, but it was just one
night. Love and commitment don't materialize because two people
spend the night together." Number three: People should be open
and honest in sexual relationships. Dad advises: "Only by opening
yourself up like this can you ever hope to, to experience the

132

exhiliration, the joy of loving another person. Now, maybe next time you won't get hurt, maybe you will, I don't now. But, uh, I think it's worth taking the risk."

Dad and son decide that the whole thing was a good learning experience, and that the boy ought to try it again with the older woman. What is the message to our youth? *Sex is a game and marriage is an unpopular option.*

*Little Darlings,* aired by RCA-owned NBC, concerned two girls in their early teens who stage a contest to see who can be the first to "make it" with a guy at summer camp. Other children in the camp choose sides and make bets on which will win. The girls range in ages from ten to fourteen or fifteen.

Angel, one of the girls in the contest, and Ferris, the other girl, set out on their missions to win the contest by being the first to "become a woman." Ferris chooses a camp counselor as her target. Angel chooses a guy from across the lake. Angel fails on her first attempt. She gets her prospective bedmate drunk but cannot follow through. Later she tries again, but chickens out, and her boyfriend promptly tells her where to go. Third time is the charm, and Angel succeeds. Success is due in part to her friend's encouraging words, "Lillies that fester smell far worse than weeds." Angel, however, finds the experience to be not at all what she had imagined, and elects not to tell any of the girls except Ferris. Ferris, on the other hand, strikes out, but claims to have had success with the counselor, and is declared winner of the contest by the other children.

Following a lengthy conversation between Ferris and Angel, in which each confesses her deeds, the girls decide the whole thing was a big mistake. They acknowledge their acts to the camp director in order to clear the counselor of any indiscretion. Decisions are made by several of the girls that sexual involvement is a personal matter not to be decided under peer pressure.

The movie ended on a positive note. But the ending could not compensate for what had gone before. The production's endless parade of vulgar, irreverent, disrespectful children surely will take its toll as little girls emulate the role models of the movie.

## Twisted Morals

*First Affair*—the title tells the story as well as any title could. But the CBS movie, aired in prime-time, twists traditional morals to conform to network television's humanist and hedonistic approach to life.

We've seen it over and over on the networks: teenager falls in love with older man; they have an affair; she declares her love; his wife discovers the affair; he goes back to his wife; teenager is heartbroken but recovers and realizes it was a good, growing-up experience.

Toby, the teen, is a country girl from Nebraska who goes to Harvard on a scholarship. She is employed by her female English professor to baby-sit and promptly falls in love with the professor's husband. The movie builds a warm and tender relationship, complete with semiexplicit scenes, between the innocent country girl and her gentle, loving, *married* older man.

The entire story carefully avoids a moral angle. In fact, Toby's liberal Harvard friends are quite supportive. Her roommate, Kathy, recommends an older man as a "good way to deal with virginity." When she learns that Toby's lover is the husband of their English professor, Kathy is upset not because of who the man is, but because Toby had kept it secret from her.

Toby feels no remorse for her sexual misconduct, only fear, saying, "I feel guilty. I mean, *not* when I'm with him, but . . . I'm afraid to go to class." Another friend shares great admiration for Toby, telling her she envies her because she takes chances. After her lover goes back to his wife, Toby deals with her broken heart with a sudden decision to leave school. After a brief, healing visit at home in Nebraska, she returns to Harvard and has a woman-to-woman talk with the understanding wife of her lover. The implication is that everybody will live happily ever after.

Sexual promiscuity is promoted as a tremendous experience, fidelity in marriage is scorned; and the humanists have preached another sermon via network television. This constant preaching of sexual immorality as being good and redemptive by the networks is taking a toll on our society. You can see the toll in broken homes and broken lives. And the silence of the church in response to it all is also heartbreaking.

### Like Father Like Son?

ABC's "Hotel" featured a segment in which a father arranged for his teenage son to have sex with a prostitute. As the program opens, Dad is saying, "This is a very sepcial weekend we're on here, Son. You might call it a rite of passage." As the plot develops, the viewer discovers that the father has arranged for his son to meet the hooker so that she can teach him to have sex without fear. It turns out that this is an old family tradition. The grandfather had arranged for the boy's father to have his first sexual experience with a Mexican prostitute when he also was sixteen.

When the son objects, Dad reassures him: "We both know it's what you want, Ronnie." To the boy's second objection, Dad responds: "It's like driving a new car. You spend a little money for the best, but you get the smoothest ride in town." Again the boy hesitates, but then decides that Dad is right and he'll feel better when it's over.

What follows is a failed attempt at sex with the hooker because the boy is turned off at the prospect of going to bed with one of Dad's old friends. When all else fails, the hooker, Claire, decides that the boy just needs someone younger. Another date is arranged for Ronnie with a younger prostitute. When Ronnie looks for the prostitute in the hotel restaurant, he picks up a girl who turns out to be a member of the vice squad. The son and father are arrested.

The program ends with reconciliation between father and son. Dad asks the son's forgiveness for trying to make him like himself.

Because the program ends on a conciliatory note, it is easy to miss the fact that here is another in a long list of network programs dealing with the subject of adult-child sex.

The curious twist is that the boy really *is* experienced, having had sex with his girlfriend. But wanting to protect the girl, he had elected not to tell Dad. Nowhere is it suggested that sex outside marriage is wrong. Nowhere is it suggested that adult-child sex is wrong. Nowhere is it suggested that there are absolutes of right and wrong governing human sexuality. Another sermon has ended.

### Networks Even Use Children's Programs to Teach

The networks also use children's programs to preach their humanist sex sermons to our children. RCA/NBC used one of its children's programs, "Silver Spoons," to exploit children and encourage them—yes, encourage preteen children—to explore sex. The episode was, of course, presented as comedy.

"Silver Spoons" is produced in association with Embassy TV, owned by Norman Lear. Lear is forever looking for something new to do in television. He stated in *USA Today* that "In the last four years . . . the world has turned 120 degrees, if not 180 degrees. There's more to write about." Lear describes television as the "most exciting medium in the world" for sharing ideas with millions of people.

The setting for the "Silver Spoons" program was a Chicago hotel where two boys were attending a Boy Scout-type convention. Twelve-year-old Ricky and his friend, Derek, attempt to trade rock concert tickets for sex with some older cheerleaders.

When Ricky tells his father about the dates, his father says, "Nice going, Son, you're a chip off the old block." Following the rock concert, Derek asks one of the girls, "Do we leave now or do we get naked?" These are twelve-year-olds!

What kind of emotion is inspired by a program where twelve-year-olds are looking for cheap sex, especially when the primary audience for the production is other adolescents? Norman Lear called it humor.

But the TV powers not only use their medium to preach their humanist sex sermons, they also use it to exploit. "Network television slinks to a historic low point," was the way John Carman of the *Atlanta Journal* described the ABC movie, *The Making of a Male Model*. Carman went on to state that producer Aaron Spelling helped to take it to this new low.

Carman said of the program that it "is the movie that breaks the slime barrier. It is to programming what cyanide is to proper diet. . . . *The Making of a Male Model* is no showcase for either talent or intelligence. It is the most brazen example yet of television beefcake. *The Making of a Male Model* isn't innocent fun. Nor is it a harmless chance to admire attractive people. It's television at its worst. It's demeaning. It's crass exploitation, and it stinks.

"Perhaps the slimiest aspect of all is that it hypocritically pretends to cluck its tongue at the very thing it exploits. The viewer is supposed to come out of the movie decrying male sexploitation, after wallowing in it for two hours."

Carman wasn't alone in his opinion of the movie. Tom Shales of the extremely liberal *Washington Post* had a similar reaction. "The film is so preposterous at every turn that it becomes the limp sort of fun that ghastly TV can be," Shales said. Shales called the executive producers Aaron Spelling and Douglas S. Cramer "tireless polluters of mainstream entertainment." Spelling has produced "Charlie's Angels," "Matt Houston," "The Love Boat," and "Hotel," among others.

Almost every avenue of prurient interest was explored in the RCA/NBC movie, *Sessions*. *The Hollywood Reporter* expressed surprise that NBC issued no parental advisory, despite the prime-time scheduling of such questionable subject matter. The movie dealt primarily with the sexual prowess of Leigh Churchill, a high-priced prostitute—hardly appropriate for prime-time family viewing. The final two minutes of the program centers on the decision of Ms. Churchill to leave the life of prostitution.

But the remainder of two hours was taken up with an endless

parade of bed scenes, in what appeared to be an attempt by NBC to reduce sex to a cheap animal commodity. References to lesbianism, group sex, and sadomasochism flowed freely from start to finish.

At one point, Ms. Churchill is describing to her therapist a "session" with one of her clients: "He's a professor—teaches electronics. And he invented some widget, component, or whatever. Anyway, he's eminent in his field. And somewhere along the way he tied sex up with being a dog. . . . I do it all. . . . He finds it necessary to repeat every couple of weeks. . . . It doesn't repel me." The movie's appeal was to the very basest elements of man's nature. But perhaps that is what NBC had in mind.

Reviewer Richard Hack called it a video wart, a sorry sight, a garbage heap, and a network crime. NBC billed it as "America's top-rated entertainment series." Both were referring to RCA/NBC's situation comedy, "We Got It Made." In describing the season opener, Hack wrote: "A grander waste of national airtime, we'd be hard pressed to locate. The new half-hour show from executive producer Fred Silverman is more than stupid; more than sexist; more than unfunny. It is at best a trashy bit of nonsense which speaks to the lowest common denominator of human flesh. And unfortunately, that's exactly what the producers had in mind."

Ordinarily, the networks would stereotype such a critic as a rightwing, fundamentalist, self-appointed censor. But Richard Hack is regular columnist for the liberal-left *Hollywood Reporter,* so he escaped those charges.

The program lived up to its billing. The first episode, written by Laura Levine, included: a strip tease and accompanying one-liners; a woman sitting nude with newspaper covering breasts and pubic area; an aerobics class designed to "limber up" one of the girls for later activity with one of the guys; and jokes dealing almost exclusively with sex.

## No Graphic Details Spared

A woman in bed describing in graphic detail the sexual content of an X-rated movie—yes, you did see that on network television. On one episode of NBC's "Bay City Blues," a man and woman were shown in bed in a hotel room. She was aroused and he was tired and trying to get to sleep. So the woman turned on the cable porno station to a movie called *High School Stewardesses.* In an attempt to stimulate her sleepy companion, the woman began vividly and graphically describing sex acts the teenage girls were performing on a man.

NBC entertainment president Brandon Tartikoff had promised

that "Bay City Blues" would show "daring and different things between men and women." Everything published prior to the season premiere of the series referred to "Bay City Blues" with terms like "bold," "creative," and "grown-up"—secular media words for indecent, crude, and morally lacking.

One episode of "St. Elsewhere" included a kinky, sexual bondage scene intended to be funny. In the scene, a woman asks her prospective lover to tie her to the bedposts. Reviewer Fred Rothenberg of the Associated Press called her "wholesomely innocent" and agreed with the show's creators that the idea is a good one for comedy.

Indeed, the attitude of the networks toward sex can clearly be seen in the process NBC uses to select their leading male characters. Just how does NBC decide on a leading male for any of its programs? Brandon Tartikoff explained in an interview with *Playboy* magazine: "I make all my final decisions (about selecting leading male characters) with the help of a trio of very discriminating 'man watchers' who work at NBC in secretarial capacities. When the time comes to cast a leading man in a series, I troop the three of them into my office and ask, 'Would you want to go to bed with this guy?' " Tartikoff is a perfect example of the typical mentality and morality of the networks.

Then there are the advertisements. Sex is used to sell everything from cars to crackers, from hair care products to hand lotion. Why do women talk to little men in toilet bowls? According to Joyce Kilbourne, it's part of the unreal world created by television advertisers in which women are slightly demented, forever young, flawlessly beautiful, and dangerously thin.

Kilbourne sees sexual stereotyping as a major problem in advertising. *Adweek* magazine featured an interview in which she discussed some sexual stereotypes in advertising. The first is the "superwoman image." Remember the Enjoli perfume commercial? "She can bring home the bacon, fry it up in a pan, and never let him forget he's a man." According to Kilbourne, the superwoman ideal erodes a woman's self-confidence by projecting a lifestyle that she can't possibly attain.

The "Gentlemen Prefer Hanes" commercial was given as an example of ads which encourage women to compete against each other by flaunting their sexuality. The ads were also labeled insulting to men because of the implication that their relationships with women are so trivial that they can be disrupted by a prettier pair of legs. Kilbourne concluded by saying, "As a model for adult intimacy, this harms all of us, women and men." Joyce Kilbourne is right.

Television has done more to misuse and teach the misuse of God's gift of sex than any other medium in the history of mankind. The examples in this chapter have only skimmed the surface.

## DISCUSSION AND REFLECTION QUESTIONS

1. Do you agree that the networks use their programs to promote the humanist view of sex?
2. Have you seen a network program in which adultery is presented as being a sin?
3. Do you think the networks help shape children's attitudes toward sex?
4. Why are so many people, depicted as Christians, shown committing adultery on television?
5. Does the constant repetition of sexual immorality have an effect on those who view it?
6. Were you surprised at the method by which the president of NBC entertainment said he selected his network's leading male characters?
7. How many products can you name which use sex in advertising to sell the product?

# NINE

# ACCORDING TO THE MEDIA, HOMOSEXUALITY IS GAY

The *Journal of Communication,* published by the University of Pennsylvania's Annenberg School of Communication, reported that, according to the networks, homosexuals are the most effective and well-organized of the many special interest groups who lobby the television entertainment industry.

Leading the pressure in behalf of presenting favorable impressions of homosexuals on television is the National Gay Task Force (NGTF). The homosexuals have groups who lobby in both New York and Hollywood, and work closely with the writers, producers, and network officials in programs dealing with homosexuals.

According to the report, the homosexuals also have 200 or so small local homosexual groups located in communities throughout the country. When acting in cooperation with the National Gay Task Force, these community-based groups form a kind of "network," similar to the television networks. The report said that "for special emergency mail distribution of crucial information relating to television programming, the NGTF has created what it calls the 'Gay Media Alert Network' which consists of 'affiliates' in cities throughout the United States."

The homosexual representatives present themselves to the networks as an "education lobby," seeking to educate media decision-makers. The report stated that much of their activity is to change the attitudes of the networks toward homosexual issues.

Reporting on the success of the homosexuals and their acceptance by the networks, the report said: "The relationship between the gay media activists and the networks has become institutionalized and informal. . . . All participants are on a first-name basis with one another. There is a routine, friendly nature to the pressure process. . . . Network decision-makers often solicit comments from gay activist leaders."

The report went on to say that "there is evidence that the networks consult regularly with gay activists on projects they are considering and that they solicit substantial input from the Gay Media Task Force in writing and producing the programs." The report also stated that, in some cases, outside approval by the homosexual community had to be obtained before the project could get beyond script stage.

The influence of homosexuals and the sympathy the media has for them was evident in *Time* and *Newsweek* reviews of *La Cage Aux Folles*, a Broadway play glamorizing homosexuality.

Phrases like "model marriage," "values of love, honor, and fidelity to home and family," and "traditional values" leap from the reviews. *Time* and *Newsweek* magazines were only two of the many media sources singing the praises of the production with abundant superlatives.

ABC's Barbara Walters, usually sharp-tongued and demanding, stepped down from her normal role as probing adversary when she interviewed homosexual Harvey Fierstein, writer of *La Cage*, on "20/20."

According to *TV Guide*, NBC is developing a TV movie about AIDS (Acquired Immune Deficiency Syndrome) and its devastating effects on the homosexual population. Says NBC senior vice-president Perry Lafferty, "This is not a gay show. . . . It's about a family. . . . " NBC was also sounding out Fierstein about writing, and perhaps starring in, a homosexual sitcom pilot for TV.

An interesting sidelight to the whole *La Cage* affair is that every review we read made specific references to the derogatory treatment of the show's one "Christian" couple. They are called uptight "religious fanatics." The man is called "France's own Jerry Falwell" and the mother does what one reviewer called a degrading bump-and-grind routine in her underwear.

*Newsweek* magazine joined the bandwagon with "Gay America: Sex, Politics, and the Impact of AIDS," an incredible piece of journalism. Covering nine pages, the articles never once gave the slightest hint that for millions homosexuality might be a moral issue.

In the fall of 1983, the Alliance for Gay Artists Awards honored Phil Donahue for the third straight year. Wendy Roth, accepting the award, said, "We hope to continue to give you the kind of attention you've given us." Alliance Chairman Chris Uszler spoke of the progress of the last three years, of multiplying membership, increased influence, and credibility. Uszler proudly noted that homosexuals were enjoying greater interaction with the entertainment industry.

The drive of TV's elite to bring about social reform has incredible potential. It is dramatically illustrated in the positive coverage of homosexuality.

### Homosexuals Have "Model" Marriage

Reviews of *La Cage Aux Folles* imply that homosexuality is in reality an all-American institution finally finding its place in the sun. The stage production is the story of two aging homosexuals raising the son whom one of them fathered years earlier in a one-night-fling with a showgirl. And the national media calls it a model marriage!

The show's composer, Jerry Herman (of *Mame* and *Hello, Dolly!* fame), says he has been accused of dealing with Mom and apple pie. Herman perverted the sacred concept of motherhood by writing a "Mom-type" song in which Mother is a man! The show's creators think it will be the most popular song in the show and will be sung at weddings and bar mitzvahs everywhere.

ABC's Hugh Downs introduced Barbara Walters' "20/20" interview with author Fierstein by proclaiming *La Cage* as a show dealing with "such traditional values as 'Honor thy father and thy mother,' and the sanctity of a long-term monogamous relationship." In the interview, Walters asks if it is rare for homosexuals to have long relationships. "No. No. It's the norm," insists Fierstein.

Despite the incredible claims of homosexual normalcy, the most striking aspect of the "20/20" interview was Walters' quiet, attentive stance. Her questions were calm, measured, and apparently never triggered by Fierstein's claims and inconsistencies. While most of Walters' subjects have to be armed to defend and/or vindicate themselves, Fierstein had nothing to fear.

He said, "I assume that everyone is gay" and less than a minute later, "I'm not attracted to heterosexual men." There was no challenge to this contradiction from the reticent Walters.

Fierstein also acknowledged being attracted to Clark Gable, saying, "I was Vivian Leigh. And so, I might have taken those characteristics of the effeminate because that was the only role model I had." At another point in the interview, he launched into a lengthy discourse on the premise that homosexuality is normal. Again, no challenge.

He said: "I've never heard of a family without a gay member

... a gay cousin or something down the line." And again, no query or challenge. It does indeed appear that Barbara Walters risked her well-earned reputation for getting to the heart of the issues she probes in her interviews. Walters brought the interview to a close with the following exchange:

WALTERS: In *La Cage Aux Folles,* the big number that closes the first act is when the transvestite, having been rejected, comes out and sings. . . .

FIERSTEIN (interrupting): Well, they tell him they don't want him.

WALTERS: Yes, and he says. . . .

FIERSTEIN (again interrupting): And he says, "I am what I am, I don't want praise. I don't want pity. I bang my own drum. Some think it's noise, I think it's pretty. There's one life, and there's no return and no deposit, one life, so it's time to open up your closet. Life ain't worth a d— till you can say, 'Hey, world, I am what I am!' "

The scene ends with Walters back at the newsdesk with Downs. She makes this final summary statement: "And Hugh, the song 'I Am What I Am,' written, incidentally, by Jerry Herman, not only expresses what homosexuals feel. But more importantly, it represents the deepest yearnings in all of us, to be loved and accepted and respected for what we are."

Hollywood's own "industry bible," the *Hollywood Reporter,* pointed out the obvious fact that Walters and Fierstein carefully avoided hot topics—the AIDS epidemic, for example. One doesn't really have to wonder what ABC was trying to accomplish with this one-sided journalism.

### Slanted Coverage

Another of the *Newsweek* articles in the issue mentioned earlier featured slanted coverage of the homosexual predicament in relationship to AIDS. Entitled "Gay America in Transition," the story began with a vivid description of the Hot House, a homosexual pleasure palace filled with the paraphernalia of kinky sex—harnesses, chains, and shackles. They pictured a young man in despair sifting through the chains and shackles and lamenting, "Not only is this over—it's all over."

Was the intent to focus attention on the AIDS epidemic, a concern to all Americans? Or was it an attempt to picture homosexuality as an approved and acceptable lifestyle?

The slant of the article verifies the Lichter-Rothman study in which they interviewed 240 journalists and broadcasters, including some from *Newsweek*. They found that of those interviewed, only 9 percent have a strong belief that homosexuality is wrong.

Studies have failed to prove that homosexuality is genetically based. However, *Newsweek* had this to say about the cause: "What seems fairly certain, given the limits of existing research, is that human sexual orientation is determined very early in life—perhaps by the age of one or two, and certainly before the child has any capacity to make a reasoned decision."

Toward the end of the article, *Newsweek* quoted Michael John of San Francisco, who said, "I sort of miss talking about the good times, going with friends to the bath houses and spending an evening, just the casualness of it." It was mentioned in the next sentence that John had at least one sexual encounter a day for nineteen years, most of them anonymous. That's almost 7,000 sex acts with people, most of whom he did not know.

However, nowhere in the article was there the slightest hint that the writers of *Newsweek* considered homosexuality to be wrong or deviant behavior. "The mass media may not be successful in telling us *what* to think," said Bernard Cohen, "but they are stunningly successful in telling us what to think about."

The danger comes when we think *about* something so long that it becomes a part of our subconscious thought processes and we forget the moral issues involved.

NBC pushed the acceptance of homosexuality in an episode of its program, "Gimme A Break," produced by Mort Lachman and Sy Rosen. Remember, Lachman and Rosen used the same sitcom to push the acceptance of pornographic magazines. The personalities of two men were probed in the program. One is angry, narrow, bigoted, prejudiced, and simpleminded. He is Carl, the *straight* police chief. The other is intellegent, sensitive, dignified, serious-minded, hardworking, and heroic. He is Jerry, the homosexual cop.

The two men are thrown together one night in a stakeout. Unaware of his friend's homosexuality, Carl cracks a joke about a "pansy" and his dog. Jerry counters with several quick Polish jokes. The chief is startled.

JERRY: What's the matter, Carl, don't you think that's funny?
CARL: Well, of course not. I'm Polish.
JERRY: That's why I don't like gay jokes.
CARL: Because you're Polish?
JERRY: No, Carl. I'm gay." (Scene ends with canned applause.)

The next scene begins with the chief obviously attempting to avoid any further conversation on the veteran officer's homosexuality. When pressed on the subject, the chief responds angrily.

CARL: How the h— can you be gay?

JERRY: How the h— can you be Polish?

CARL: Because my grandparents came from Poland. But even if your grandparents came from San Francisco, that's still no excuse.

JERRY: Carl, I don't need an excuse to be what I am.

Later in the conversation the chief raises the question of the officer's former marriage. Jerry answers, "Yeah, I was married, I had a kid. The marriage was a big mistake; the kid wasn't. I'm gay, Carl; I like being gay. I'm happy being gay. I'm a gay gay."

The drama intensifies as the officer attempts to enlighten his superior on the "real world."

JERRY: Carl, you better get used to it. A lot of things have changed. There are gay doctors, gay lawyers, gay firemen, and gay cops.

CARL: I may be prejudiced, bigoted, and, and, and old-fashioned . . . but you gotta admit that there's something about gay people that's different.

JERRY: Like what?

CARL: From *normal* people.

JERRY: Oh, you mean Adolf Hitler, Charlie Manson, Son of Sam. What the h— have you got against gays? You know what you are? You're a homophobe.

CARL: A what?

JERRY: It means "homophobia," an unnatural fear of homosexuals.

What follows is an amazing bit of character manipulation designed to draw sympathy for homosexuality. In what *seems* a contradiction of all he has said, Carl tells a pitiful story of his early childhood.

CARL: Let me tell you a story. . . . As a kid I wasn't the warm, open, loving guy that I am today. . . . I had this stammer, and the other kids used to kid me because of it. But this one English teacher named Mr. Lamet, he kinda took a shine to me. Afternoons I stayed after school and he worked with me, readin' out loud. And after a while the stutter practically disappeared. Anyway, one night, Uncle Joey comes home real late shoutin' about how the cops had busted Mr. Lamet in some gay bar.

JERRY (interrupting): Good-bye, Mr. Chips.

CARL: Next day at school they said that Mr. Lamet had the flu. Well, all the kids snickered and laughed. Everybody knew. You can't keep a secret like that in a small town. I never saw Mr. Lamet after that.

JERRY: He moved out of town?

CARL: No, he crashed his car into a tree. Uncle Joey wouldn't let me go to the funeral. He said that if anybody saw me, the whole town would think that me and Mr. Lamet were boyfriends or something. Anyway, I didn't go. Maybe I was afraid that people would talk too. I don't know.

JERRY (reaching the wrong conclusion): Carl, thanks for sharin' that with me.

CARL: What do you mean?

JERRY: I mean, I'm impressed that you would understand what your Uncle Joey didn't.

CARL (shouting): Boy, you people twist everything around to your own point of view, don't you? Well, you're the one who's wrong. Everything I learned, I learned from my Uncle Joey. It's because of him that I didn't grow up to be one, to be one of you.

JERRY: Wait a minute, Carl.

CARL: No, no, now you wait a minute. You listen to me. When Uncle Joey was dyin', they let us kids in to see him one by one. He even died like a man. We didn't hug; we didn't kiss. He just closed his eyes and went. And I just watched him. Don't you say anything about Uncle Joey, God rest his soul." (The chief storms out of the room.)

The chief gets locked in the men's room and Jerry responds to a call. Jerry heroically confronts the criminal and is wounded in a shootout. After the chief has time to reflect on the events, he comes home and finds his housekeeper still up awaiting some word from the stakeout. Carl states that the mission has been successful but that Jerry has been wounded in the process.

As the program ends, the chief declares with emotion, "Boy, that Jerry is one h__ of a guy."

How is it that both the advocate *and* the adversary are cast in roles which support the homosexual cause? The advocate, in this case a practicing homosexual, presents an intelligent, logical, persuasive, and emotional case. The adversary, the chief, opposes homosexuality, but his argument is predictably deficient. He presents his case in such an irrational, mindless, inconsistent manner that any thinking person would reject both the argument and the person. This has become an effective formula for the transmission of values through network television.

## Those Opposing Homosexuality Are Negatively Stereotyped

On one edition of ABC's "Dynasty," Blake Carrington (Daddy) is suing for custody of his grandson, hoping to prove that the boy's homosexual father (his own son) is unfit. It is an increasingly familiar and predictable pattern. The homosexual is cast in the best possible manner, while the person (or persons) opposed to homosexuality is shown to be ignorant, prejudiced, unethical, and exhibiting an array of undesirable personality traits.

"Dynasty" is no exception. Blake Carrington, ironfisted ruler of the family, takes the witness stand to be cross-examined by his son Stephen's lawyer.

LAWYER: Do you consider yourself to be a prejudiced man, Mr. Carrington?

BLAKE: As I understand the word, no.

LAWYER: Would you please share your understanding of the word "prejudice" with the court?

BLAKE: It's an opinion based on ignorance.

LAWYER: Tell me, Mr. Carrington, have you met many homosexuals?

BLAKE: A few.

LAWYER: Do you have any friends who are homosexual?

BLAKE: Not to my knowledge.

LAWYER: Any working for you?

BLAKE: None that I am aware of personally.

LAWYER: What if you were aware? Would you do anything about it?

BLAKE: If their lifestyle didn't interfere with their work or with me, no.

LAWYER: In other words, as long as they stay clear of Blake Carrington, it's fine. . . . You have a large circle of so-called straight friends?

BLAKE: I'd like to think so, yes.

LAWYER: Are some of them honest, some not? Does one maybe cheat on his wife while another's a model family man? Do some drink too much? In short, Mr. Carrington, do you find in your straight world that individuals vary from man to man?

BLAKE: Yes, of course.

LAWYER (shouting): Then why do you have this blind prejudice against homosexuals?

Later in the trial, Krystle, Blake's current wife, testifies in Stephen's behalf. When asked why Stephen should be considered an appropriate father, she says, "Because I've experienced his gentleness, understanding, and tolerance." She goes on to describe how she and Blake had taken in the grandson when it was supposed that

Stephen was dead. But when he was found to be alive, Krystle stated her feelings about the child living with his homosexual father: "Knowing that Danny would grow up with Stephen's warmth and tenderness, I knew it was the best thing in the world for both of them." Beautiful, moving music accompanied her testimony.

## Same Pattern Is Used in Other Programs

This same pattern was followed in an episode of "Cheers." Written and produced by Ken Levine and David Isaacs (remember their anti-Christian episode of "AfterMASH"?), the comedy involves a bar owner, Sam, whose friend has written a book in which he "comes out of the closet." Unaware of the book's content, Sam invites his friend (Tom) to have a press conference at Sam's bar to kick off sales for the book.

During the press conference, the issue of Tom's homosexuality is raised. Sam is caught by surprise and hastily exits for a conference with one of the waitresses, Diane.

SAM: I just can't believe it. I mean the guy was a hound, Diane. He had women everywhere. We'd go on the road, we'd go into hotel lobbies. There'd be three, four women holdin' up kids.

DIANE: He covers that, he covers that.

SAM: Where?

DIANE: Here, here in this paragraph, here.

SAM (reading aloud from book): From the outside, my days of baseball seemed glorious. But the greater my fear became of my true sexuality, the more I compensated with typical Don Juan promiscuity.

DIANE: Does that explain it?

SAM: I don't know. I've only read it once.

DIANE: He was denying who he was. He's no longer doing that. (Sam moves across the room and Diane follows.)

DIANE: Sam, I do understand why you're upset. You're afraid that now people will think that you're . . .

SAM: I'm not upset. I'm not upset. It's just that guys should be guys, Diane. That's all.

DIANE: Sam, look. Your friend Tom's out there. He needs your support now more than ever before. He really hasn't changed, you know. He's still the same guy you used to tinkle off balconies with.

SAM: Boy, the world was a lot simpler then, you know.

Tom enters and apologetically declares: "Sam, I'm sorry about all this. See, I thought you'd read the book and everything was cool.

Look, I don't want to cause you any more problems, so I'm just going to take off, OK?" Sam rushes out after his old buddy and embraces him. Photographs are taken by newsmen on the scene. When the pictures appear the following morning in local papers, bar patrons fear that the place will become a hangout for homosexuals.

Sam enters the bar where several customers are examining the picture in the news.

MAN AT BAR (Norm): Er, um, I'm looking at your kisser in the morning write-up here, Sam.

DIANE: Every time I look at this, I feel proud of you, Sam.

SAM: Yeah, I'm kinda glad I did that now.

DIANE: I think you are taking real strides in your development as a human being.

SAM: You know, a couple of other chicks said that to me today. I think this, uh, human being image is gonna get me more action than cheap wine. . . . Hey, Norm, what was that you said yesterday about Vitto's pub?

NORM: All right, you've heard about Vitto's pub?

SAM: It's a gay bar, right?

NORM: It didn't used to be. It used to be a great bar. . . . One night Vitto lets a gay group hold a meeting in the back room, right? Gays for the metric system, or something. Story got in the newspaper, gets a lot of attention, the next thing you know Vitto's pub turns into *Vitto's Pub* (said effeminitely). All the regulars left, Sammy. . . .

SAM: I don't believe that stuff. Bars don't turn gay overnight.

DIANE: Excuse me. You're talking about them like they're a bunch of ogres. The fact of the matter is, there are gay people in this bar all the time.

Diane goes on to add that there are two gays in the bar at that very moment. At this point, the regulars begin a frantic search to discover the two in question. Two men approach the bar and order light beers. The regulars decide to test the two by shouting, "Hey look at the baganzas on that babe." The two men fail to look up. Diane approaches and says in a deep cowboylike voice, "Well, they're not watchin'. Let's string 'em up."

Carla, another waitress, is concerned.

CARLA: What are we gonna do about these guys, huh?

DIANE: Carla, you're not prejudiced against gays, are you?

CARLA: Well, I'm not exactly crazy about 'em. I mean, I get enough competition from women. I'm tellin' ya, if guys keep comin' outa the closet, there isn't gonna be anybody left to date, and

I'm gonna have to start goin' out with girls.

The regulars decide to leave for a nearby bar.

SAM: You guys are kidding, right?

NORM: Um, Sammy, we'll check in, in a couple of weeks and we'll just see if Cheers is still the kind of bar where a single woman can be assured of being harrassed and hit on.

SAM: Get back here, all of you, right now. You mean to tell me that you guys are bailing out on me?

MAN AT BAR: Sam, I'm telling you, within a month, there's gonna be wild music and guys dancin' and exchanging phone numbers.

Following a general uproar, Sam decides to ask the supposed homosexuals to leave. He asks Diane's advice about what to say. She replies, "Oh, well, it's very simple. You just walk up and say, 'Hello, we're a bunch of sniveling bigots, and, uh, we don't care for your kind.'" Sam reconsiders and orders beers on the house for the alleged homosexuals.

Regular patrons trick the newcomers into believing the bar is closing. The men leave and the regulars return. As they laugh and congratulate themselves, Diane walks back to the bar and says, "Norman, I think there is something you should know about those guys. They're not gay. In fact, one of them tried to hit on me tonight. . . . I said there were two gay men in the bar. I didn't say who they were. They, along with myself, have had a wonderful time watching you make complete idiots of yourselves. Yeah, the guys I was talking about are still here. Right guys?" At this point, two men (the real homosexuals) bend over and kiss Norm on the cheeks. Norm points to one and says that the kiss is "better than Vera's" (Norm's wife). The program ends.

## Repetition Helps Reinforce the Sermon

By repeating the same "sermon," the networks reinforce the "rightness" of homosexuality. Another example is found in an episode of NBC's hospital drama, "St. Elsewhere."

"St. Elsewhere" dealt with AIDS with only one hint that there might be a moral issue involved, but that possibility was quickly discarded. The program was anxious to present homosexuality as acceptable in today's "enlightened" society and never proposed that one's suffering from AIDS could be the consequence of an act which defies the laws of nature and of God. (There is still a great deal unknown about AIDS, but it *is* known that the disease—which breaks down the body's immune systems and usually results in death—is most often suffered by those active in homosexual practice.) In fact, one of the doctor's comments imply a bitterness toward the "unfairness" of a situation which brings suffering to one because he chooses a deviant lifestyle.

The "St. Elsewhere" AIDS victim is Tony Gifford, a popular, young, Boston city councilman who has a wife and son. In a confrontation with his wife, Gifford denies any homosexual involvement. Unconvinced, his wife storms from his hospital room in tears.

A hospital staff member, who is also a personal friend of the Giffords, urges him to "go public" because "you're a popular figure. If you went public, you could have Boston coming up with new funding for AIDS research. This doesn't necessarily have to hurt your career."

Following a brief argument between the staff member and Gifford, she again encourages Gifford to be "truly honest." Gifford replies, "Oh, you want honesty. . . . you want truth. It *was* men, it was men. I never even knew their names."

. The concluding scene in the episode features three hospital administrative staff members commenting on the Gifford case and overtly stating NBC's intent to minimize the real issues in the AIDS phenomenon. The following dialogue occurs in that final scene:

DR. WESTPHAL: You know, I keep coming back to Tony Gifford. He's a young man. Now what's going to happen to him in the time he has left?

HELEN: I don't know. Maybe he should have thought about that sooner.

DR. WESTPHAL: Yeah, I know. That's how I felt about it at first. And then I started to think—who am I? Why should any of us be penalized fatally for choosing a certain lifestyle? Especially when you realize that it all boils down to chance anyway. And I tell you something! I don't give a d__ for all this talk about morality. . . .

Having determined that AIDS has no moral implications, the good doctors quickly turn to lighter topics.

DR. CRANE: OK, come on. I'll treat you to a triple B.

HELEN: What?

DR. CRANE: BBB—"beat the blues bourbon!"

The three laugh as one. In congenial agreement that booze will surely solve their problems, Westphal and Helen rise to join Crane. Leaving the office, the hospital, Councilman Gifford, and AIDS, (that is, *all* their problems and worries) behind, they depart secure in the knowledge that the bottle will cure all ills.

## NBC Lies about Homosexuality on "Love, Sidney"

When NBC announced its series, "Love, Sidney," the network released the following statement: "With particular regard to 'Love, Sidney,' we would point out that it is not about homosexuality .... The series itself does not take its theme from any particular lifestyle." The final episode of "Love, Sidney" showed how convenient it is for the networks to lie when it is to their advantage.

In the season's finale, Sidney went out with a "wham." "Wham" is the word in the program that Sidney uses to describe his feelings for a young woman. He refuses to call it love because it cannot be reconciled with his homosexuality. The program centers on these conflicting emotions.

The drama begins with the company boss, Jason, offering Sidney an advertising contract which demands almost-round-the-clock work for two weeks. Sidney's assistant is Allison, a beautiful woman with whom Jason is romantically involved. Jason is certain that Allison will be "safe" with Sidney.

Following several preliminary lighthearted quips about Sidney's lifestyle, the program settles into what amounts to an all-out attempt to portray homosexuality as not only an approved but also a desirable alternative.

One scene has Sidney sharing his mixed emotions with the company secretary, Nancy. Sidney explains that he is developing strong feelings for someone he works with and that he is sure the feelings are reciprocated.

NANCY: My God, you and Jason have fallen in love.

SIDNEY: It's worse.

NANCY: What could be worse than Jason?

SIDNEY: A woman . . . Nancy, I'm so confused. How can I be feeling this sort of thing for a woman?

NANCY: Sidney, we talked about you and Martin (Sidney's former homosexual lover), and I know you think there will never be anyone to replace him, but I happen to believe it's possible for a leopard to change his spots.

SIDNEY: What about a pink panther? This is impossible.

Later, back at his apartment, Allison arrives intent on persuading Sidney to admit his feelings for her. She is unaware of his homosexuality. The scene is punctuated by alternate shots of Sidney gazing longingly at Allison and afterward at the picture of Martin. Sidney tries in vain to tell the woman why he cannot act on his feelings.

About this time, Jason comes to the rescue. He knocks at the apartment door and enters. While Allison is in another room, Jason explains to Sidney that Allison has left him for another man. Sidney hurriedly ushers him out of the apartment. But as he leaves, Jason offers this startling observation: "I envy you, Sidney. No kidding. Your life may be a little different, but at least you know who you are. Sidney Shorr knows who he is and what he is. You're a lucky man."

The program concludes with Sidney reaffirming his homosexuality, and now, knowing "who he is and what he is," he declares that he is "all right."

During the fall of 1983, the networks opened the doors promoting homosexuality on several other programs. CBS aired *Senior Trip*, a movie featuring as a major subplot the homosexuality of a young artist who was repeatedly assured by a fellow senior that he was normal and OK.

NBC's "Hill Street Blues" featured a veteran policeman, twice honored with medals of valor, acclaimed by all as a "good cop." He was also homosexual. When he was forced out of the closet by having to testify to a murder witnessed in a gay bar, his captain sadly declared, "They're gonna crucify him."

The CBS movie, *Trackdown*, contained a scene of a long and passionate mouth-to-mouth kiss between an older male and younger male homosexual. It was the kind of kiss one would normally expect to see between heterosexuals. Another CBS movie, *Making Love*, glamorized the affair of a married man and his lover and contained several bed scenes.

Even the ABC soap opera, "All My Children," introduced a character who is a lesbian, though the character is no longer on the program. Her profession—a child psychologist. My speculation is this: introducing a regular homosexual character into a daytime soap *and* as a child psychologist is simply one more step in the networks' intention to reshape our society.

The Lichter-Rothman report reveals that only 5 percent of the network leaders strongly feel that homosexuality is wrong. The same report reveals that two thirds of that group see their role as using TV to promote social reform. One thing they had in mind was the promotion of homosexuality.

What is the goal of the homosexuals, to whom the secular, liberal, national media is lending support? The North American Man-Boy Love Association, the organization which feels that it should not be illegal to have homosexual relations with children of any age, held its seventh annual meeting in Boston.

Charley Shively, a homosexual leader in the Boston area, speaking to the conference, said he wished to "attack a presupposition .... that parents have a hereditary right to their children, that parents have a right to their children that we homosexuals do not have."

The National Coalition of Gay Organizations has officially supported the Man-Boy Love group since 1972. The International Gay Association recently voted the group into its membership. And the New York City Community Council of Lesbian-Gay Organizers also has admitted the Man-Boy group.

The meeting of the homosexual group was held at the Arlington Street Unitarian Church in Boston. The Unitarian Church is humanist in its beliefs.

## DISCUSSION AND REFLECTION QUESTIONS

1. Have you seen a network program in which homosexuality was presented as being morally wrong?
2. Have you seen a network program in which homosexuality was presented as being morally acceptable and right?
3. Why do the networks present homosexuality in a favorable light?
4. Why are militant homosexuals so readily accepted by the networks and the national secular media?
5. Why did NBC say "Love, Sidney" was not about homosexuality and then proceed to make a positive statement concerning homosexuality in the program?
6. Do you agree with Charley Shively of the North American Man-Boy Love Association that homosexuals have equal right to your children? Why or why not?

# TEN

# IN HOLLYWOOD, IT IS SNOWING EVERY DAY

Did you ever wonder why alcohol is used so often in television programs? The answer is not all that complicated. Alcohol is very much a part of the life of those who produce the programs. When they need some "movement" in a program, alcohol is the natural object for that movement. Ben Stein, in his book *The View from Sunset Boulevard,* had something to say about the people who are responsible for our programs which fits well here. "The super-medium of television is spewing out the messages of a few writers and producers (literally in the low hundreds), almost all of whom live in Los Angeles. Televison is not necessarily a mirror of anything besides what those few people think. The whole entertainment component of television is dominated by men and women who have a unified, idiosyncratic view of life."

One need not have a long memory to recall the number of people associated with the entertainment industry who have died from a drug overdose or who have been alcoholics. It is, generally speaking, part and parcel of the industry. Therefore, the reason for the overwhelming use and approval of liquor and drugs in programs is that it reflects the values of those responsible for the programs.

Then too we need to remember the vast amount of money which the liquor industry pours into television advertising. To think that the networks are going to realistically portray the use of a product whose industry provides them with such large sums of money is naive.

According to a report from the Associated Press, prime-time television has shown a dramatic rise in on-the-air drinking during the past three decades. Researchers who sampled more than 280 hours covering three decades of television concluded that drinking is up during prime-time, but smoking is down.

Dr. Warren Breed and Dr. James R. De Foe conducted the study which was published, in part, in the *New England Journal of Medicine*. Their findings revealed that the use of alcohol on TV was unchanged until recent years. During the '50s, '60s, and '70s, TV shows depicted an average of four drinking acts per hour. But by the early '80s, this had doubled to eight drinking acts per hour.

When actor Peter Strauss told *TV Guide* about rampant cocaine abuse in Hollywood, he quoted a familiar saying in the entertainment capital: "It is snowing in Hollywood every day." Many leaders in the entertainment field claim that the use of cocaine and other illegal drugs is probably no more common among their group than among other upper-income groups around the country. They complain that TV and the press pay a disproportionate amount of attention to drug use in the entertainment world.

Others, however, including Los Angeles police chief Daryl Gates, disagree. Gates said it is appropriate to focus attention on drug use in Hollywood, not only because it is illegal and so widespread there, but also because performers become role models for young people.

## Hollywood Has Its Own Drug Code

Law enforcement officials cite two barriers to actually enforcing the law in Hollywood. One is the broad social acceptance of illicit drugs there, and the other is the code in the entertainment industry that prohibits cooperation.

A *New York Times* article on the subject reported that leaders in the field acknowledge that the use of drugs has an adverse effect on the quality and content of programming. Yet there is a strong cover-up attitude among that same group.

Dr. Thomas Radecki of the National Coalition on Television Violence stated: "With the new research in the past two years, it is increasingly clear that TV advertising and program use of alcohol is playing a major role in the increasing abuse of alcohol." Radecki said that the average child will see alcohol consumed 75,000 times on TV before he is of legal drinking age. The typical adult will view 5,000 scenes per year. Ninety-nine percent of these portrayals will be neutral or favorable. Alcohol abuse and violence are the two most rapidly rising causes of death in the United States. Fifty percent of real-life violence is associated with alcohol consumption, while only 1 percent of televised violence is presented in connection with drinking.

According to the Memphis *Commercial Appeal*, Lee Anne Read of Memphis is a worldly wise sixteen-year-old who took her first drink when she was nine. She is now a recovering alcohol and drug abuser. In an article in the newspaper, Miss Read said she started drinking because "she knew older youngsters did it and she had seen it glorified on television."

Miss Read's statement contradicted that of CBS president Gene Jankowski. Jankowski told a group of leading Southern Baptists that television did not influence anyone. Jankowski told the group: "To assume that television . . . is a kind of one-directional impact machine is to assume something which is contrary to human nature."

Jankowski said the reason television doesn't influence anyone, even TV advertising, is that "the customer makes a decision after the message is received." Jankowski did not explain how anyone could make a decision before the message is received, nor how making a decision after the message is received failed to influence people.

In the summer of 1983, the Center for Science in the Public Interest released a report on the effects of alcoholic beverage advertising. Michael Jacobson, representative of the center, summarized the study. "Our basic conclusion is that a significant amount of alcohol advertising is unfair and deceptive. . . . " He went on to say, "The alcohol industry is pouring millions of dollars a year into getting people to drink more."

The report dealt with such areas as: (1) the use of the athlete role-model in promoting alcoholic beverages; (2) the use of psychologists to adapt ads to a particular age-group; (3) ad themes which suggest that drinking contributes to a socially and professionally successful life; and (4) aiming advertisements at particularly vulnerable groups such as the young and heavy drinkers.

### Move to Remove Liquor Ads from TV Begins

The Center for Science's report fueled a move to get alcohol advertising banned from television. (Cigarette commercials were banned from radio and TV in 1971.) By the fall of 1983, a grass-roots movement had gained the necessary momentum to win the attention of Congress on the matter. Bills that would restrict alcohol advertising were introduced in at least ten states and in the House of Representatives during 1983.

Sociology professor Donald Strickland of Washington University in St. Louis said his studies show no connection whatever between alcohol advertising and alcohol abuse. Incidentally, Strickland's studies were funded by the United States Brewers' Association.

The alcohol industry said that present beer advertising is aimed at getting existing consumers to change brands, not to increase consumption. Marketing data would tend to suggest just the opposite. In the decade of the '70s, spending on TV advertising of alcohol increased 500 percent. And during the same period, consumption of wine increased by 65 percent, while consumption of beer increased by 31 percent.

Howard Blane, research psychologist at the University of Pittsburgh, said that abusive advertising is a problem, especially on the college campus. Quoted in *Advertising Age,* Blane said, "Beer companies do indeed encourage episodes of abuse, by encouraging beer-drinking contests, supplying beer for parties, suggesting in advertising that students have a beer blast after exams, and the like."

It is not hard to believe that beer companies will begin putting their ads in cartoon form in the not too distant future in order to reach young children as potential customers.

According to Dr. Kenneth Shonberg, director of adolescent medicine at Montefiore Hospital in the Bronx, the leading cause of death for adolescents in this country today is the abuse of alcohol and marijuana. At an American Medical Association conference on child and adolescent health problems, Shonberg said nearly three quarters of all high school seniors now use liquor regularly, with one third getting drunk at least once a month.

One third use marijuana frequently, with 15 to 29 percent getting dangerously high every month. Shonberg added that the leading cause of death for young people in 1979 was accidents, more than 60 percent of which were alcohol-related car accidents.

Jim Wollert, news director for WSMS-FM in Memphis, said that "boozing" and even taking drugs is considered routine in the business of broadcast journalism. Wollert told a meeting of radio-television news directors that TV news directors and reporters fit all three categories of people most likely to fall victim to alcohol and drug abuse. According to Wollert, who is also associate professor of journalism at Memphis State University, the three categories are: (1) working in a high-pressure job, (2) working in a high-pressure industry, and (3) working in a climate where drinking and taking drugs is considered an occupational prerequisite. Wollert also told of a similar danger in newspaper work, citing a recent study by *Newspaper Research Journal* which found that one out of every five persons in newspaper newsrooms is alcoholic.

The positive portrayal of liquor is having its effect. Two new Justice Department studies give more evidence of a significant link between crime and the use of alcohol and illegal drugs. It seems that about half of all inmates in state prisons throughout the United States said they had been drinking just prior to committing their offenses. One third of all inmates were under the influence of an illegal drug when they committed their crimes. That should tell us something about the need for control and law enforcement to stop the drug traffic.

Monitoring by the Coalition for Better Television indicates that approximately 76 percent of all persons shown drinking any beverage on prime-time television are shown drinking alcohol. Alcohol is the number-one drug problem in America.


DISCUSSION AND REFLECTION QUESTIONS
1. Why do the networks show so much alcohol consumption on their programs?
2. Can you remember a movie or television star who died of an overdose of drugs?
3. Why do the networks hardly ever show the consequences of drinking and drugs?
4. Do you think network officials who say television doesn't influence anyone to drink are correct?
5. Should liquor ads (including beer and wine) be banned from television as cigarette ads have been?
6. Were you aware that the leading cause of death among adolescents is the abuse of alcohol and marijuana? Do you think that movies and television have contributed to this situation?

# ELEVEN

# WHY I DON'T BELIEVE ALL I AM TOLD

Seven years ago I believed nearly everything reported on the network news programs. Not only that, but I would have denied to the death that the networks would slant their news coverage or be biased in presenting it. But about three years after founding the National Federation for Decency, I had to admit that my conclusions about network news were wrong. While some news is not slanted or biased, some of it most definitely is. When it is slanted, it is usually slanted against conservatives, especially conservative Christians.

Our examination of network programming has not included a hard look at the news. Accuracy In Media, the Washington-based organization founded by my good friend, Reed Irvine, is the authority in this area. (I recommend that you subscribe to AIM Report, 1341 G Street, N.W., Suite 312, Washington, D.C. 20005.) I have learned enough to know that the news departments at the networks are dominated by the same mentality and morality as the entertainment departments.

Give some examples, you say. Remember the Grenada incident in the fall of 1983? On October 27, all three networks aired videotapes of action on Grenada provided by the Pentagon. CBS showed its great displeasure by labeling the pictures, "Cleared by Defense Department censors," and Dan Rather said twice that they were "shot and censored by the U.S. government." The implication was that they were untrustworthy. But earlier, on August 3, CBS News used videotapes shot on the Soviet ship, the *Ulyanov*, in a Nicaraguan port to prove that President Reagan had been wrong in saying that it was carrying military equipment. Rather didn't mention that the tape was shot by a Cuban camera crew and cleared by Cuban military authorities. Commenting on the incident, Reed Irvine wrote: "Such journalists shouldn't be trusted with secrets that can mean life or death for our fighting men."

CBS News admitted ten violations of its own editorial guidelines in its documentary, "The Uncounted Enemy: A Vietnam Deception," in which Gen. William Westmoreland was accused of falsifying enemy troop strength. CBS tried to keep secret the report citing the violations, and made it public only after a court order to do so.

TV Guide carried an article concerning "The Uncounted Enemy: A Vietnam Deception." After two *TV Guide* reporters spent two months reviewing tapes and transcripts and talking with officials interviewed in the documentary, as well as with the journalists at CBS, the magazine concluded: "CBS began the project already convinced that a conspiracy had been perpetrated and turned a deaf ear toward evidence that suggested otherwise." The report went on to say that "CBS screened for one sympathetic witness—in order to persuade him to redo his on-camera interview—the statements of other witnesses already on film. But CBS never offered the targets of its conspiracy charge any opportunity, before their interviews, to hear their accusers, or to have a second chance before the cameras. . . . CBS asked sympathetic witnesses soft questions, while grilling unfriendly witnesses with prosecutorial zeal. . . . CBS pulled quotes out of context, misrepresented the accounts of events provided by some witnesses, while ignoring altogether other witnesses who might have been able to challenge CBS's assertions."

## Network News Biased Against the President

*Public Opinion* magazine evaluated the network television news treatment accorded President Reagan in January and February of 1983 and found that the President got the short end of the stick. The ratio of bad news to good news about the President was 13.5 to 1. For every one report favorable to the President, more than thirteen unfavorable reports were broadcast.

The effect was even more unfavorable because the stories that were hostile were sharply hostile, while so-called positive pieces were, at best, moderately favorable. As it turns out, the unfavorable reports ran almost 9,000 words each, the neutral reports almost 6,000 words, and the favorable reports 400 words.

Referring to their report on television news practices, *Public Opinion* is quoted as saying, " . . . the Presidency is an institution, an element of stability in our society, and the media are not interested in upholding our institutions. . . . The media are deluded by the belief that they actually are in command, and they cannot tolerate a Reagan incumbency that reminds them daily that their delusion is sick: that it is not Reagan, but they, who are 'out of touch.'"

Fred Barnes is an experienced national political reporter for the *Baltimore Sun*. He monitored the way the three network news organizations treated the Reagan administration's budget cuts. Barnes said that the network coverage is often "unbalanced, unfair, and uninformed." Barnes said the coverage of CBS "regularly emphasized the exotic, the unrepresentative, and the emotional."

Barnes cites examples of the twisted coverage. On the "CBS Evening News" on October 2, 1981, Charles Osgood reported that a budget-cutting wind has been "blowing strong enough to uproot some government programs—CETA is gone—and tear the roof off some other ones—food stamps, for example."

According to Barnes, money for food stamps actually dropped only from $11.4 billion to $11.3 billion. That is less than 1 percent. What was changed, but not reported by CBS, was that stamps now can go only to a family of four whose gross income does not exceed 130 percent of the poverty income level, or $11,000. Previously it was $14,000.

In a report from Nashville on April 9, 1982, ABC reporter Richard Threlkeld told millions of viewers that because of school lunch cuts, schools were forced "to raise the price of a hot lunch to $1.10, too high for some families." What Threlkeld didn't report, according to Barnes, was "that eligible poor still got free lunches" and that the near-poor children continued to get lunch at a greatly reduced discount.

Threlkeld said that nearly a million "lower-income children" were taken from the program. But Barnes said that Threlkeld failed to report that children "no longer entitled to free or reduced-price lunches came from families that had incomes above 185 percent of the poverty level." Barnes said to describe them simply as "lower-income children" was disingenuousness of a high order.

On February 13, 1982, NBC reporter Roger O'Neil told of a day-care center closing after one CETA-paid worker was dropped. O'Neil said nothing about the waste that CETA produced. O'Neil seemed to blame the program's end on the CETA cuts. Barnes said that "state regulations" were the reason.

Barnes said that the network news organizations leave the conclusion that "failed social programs are either rare or nonexistent." He said that the network news organizations have consistently presented the Reagan budget cuts as deep and harmful. Barnes said that "the hard evidence suggests the cuts were marginal."

## How Many People Are Responsible for "CBS News"?

If I asked you how many people are responsible for what stories you see covered on the evening news, what would you say? It might interest you to know that on the "CBS Evening News" the decision concerning which stories are covered lies in the hands of one man.

When Dan Rather was asked to fill the shoes of Walter Cronkite two years ago, he agreed to accept the position *only* if he could be managing editor as well as anchorperson. Rather was asked by editors of *Broadcasting* magazine what it was that made "CBS News" journalistically superior to ABC and NBC. He responded, "A broadcast, particularly a news broadcast, has to be somebody's decision. Somebody's got to have a vision of the news broadcast. The difference between CBS and the other two is that here, the anchorperson has that responsibility. And he's one person. It's much better if you get one person's vision than if you have something put together by a committee."

Nearly 15 percent of the viewing public get their evening news from CBS. And what they get as news is decided entirely by Dan Rather. Later in the interview with *Broadcasting* editors, the question was asked, "Do you come in in the morning and decide what stories you're going to do today?" Rather responded by saying, "Yes, that's what I do. . . . I'm trying to be directly responsible for the content." The next time you are watching the "CBS Evening News," remember that it reflects the selection and vision of one man, Dan Rather.

CBS was nervous in the spring of 1983 when Rather had to go to court in Los Angeles to defend himself against a libel suit. Rather had gone on the air with the charge that a young black doctor, Dr. Carl Galloway, had signed a false medical report that was purportedly used to collect a false insurance claim. Galloway sued Rather and CBS.

Dr. Galloway was able to demonstrate that his name had been forged on the medical report, and he denied having anything to do the with insurance scam. He testified that neither Dan Rather nor anyone from CBS had checked with him about that false medical report before Rather accused him of committing a felony before the 40 million or so viewers who watch "60 Minutes."

Rather contended that he had placed two phone calls to Dr. Galloway's office. Rather didn't hear from Galloway. Rather testified that it was his experience that the guilty generally don't call back. Dr. Galloway denied ever having received any messages.

A television journalist, Steve Wilson, working on the Galloway case for a syndicated news program, wanted to interview Rather. Wilson telephoned Rather three times. Rather didn't call back. Wilson sent him a registered letter. Still no reply. Wasn't it Rather who stated that the guilty don't call back?

Finally, Wilson resorted to a technique that "60 Minutes" had made famous—the ambush interview. He and his camera crew waited outside CBS News headquarters in New York until Dan Rather appeared. Going up to Rather, Wilson said: "Could I see you for just a moment? I've called your office three times. I've sent you a registered letter. . . . I don't know how else to do it."

Rather half-grinned, put his hand on Steve Wilson's shoulder, and said to a member of the camera crew, "Get that microphone right up, will you?" Rather then uttered a four-letter obscenity: "__ you. You got it? Clearly?"

Later, Rather realized that he might have made a mistake by his rude and vulgar conduct. He called Wilson to apologize and to offer him an interview. Rather even sent a note to Wilson: "I mistook who you were and what you were doing. That was inexcusable, rude, and un-Christian behavior for which I am remorseful." Wilson was unmoved. The program aired, but the obscenity was bleeped out. Rather was right. His behavior was, as he said, un-Christian. But, you know, we have come to expect that from the networks.

Rather was honored with St. Bonaventure University's 1983 Bob Considine award. The award is named for the reporter and broadcaster who died in 1975. The university says the award is given annually in recognition of the high moral and ethical standards that Considine stood for.

At or about the same time the award was being given, Rather was giving an in-depth interview to *Playboy*. When asked about CBS's coverage of Russia, Rather responded: "The only person I'll listen to in criticism about our coverage of the Soviet Union is Harrison Salisbury. . . . With everybody else, my attitude is '__ you.' "

At one point, Rather lamented the fact that he could no longer do much regular reporting. "But," he added, "the day I look at myself in the mirror and say, 'Listen, you're no longer a reporter; you've become something else,' that's the day I _____ guarantee you I'll walk into the office of the president of CBS News and say, 'I want to do something else.' " Rather filled in the blank here by using God's name in vain.

Later, the *Playboy* reporter asked if Rather thought it was important to keep his political views to himself. Rather stated: "I don't think people give a ___ what Dan Rather thinks about a specific issue or a specific politician . . . if you and I go out for a beer and you say, 'What do you think about Mitterand's policy in France?' and I say, 'I think he's a full-of___ socialist and I don't think his policy will work.'" I think you know what barnyard words Rather employed to fill in these blanks.

The late Robert Kennedy and I have something in common. We both refused interviews with *Playboy*. I would have thought more highly of Dan Rather if he had done the same thing.

I was not too surprised when Rather prefaced a segment on his news program dealing with the Coalition for Better Television with his prejudiced remark about a group of people "who want to tell you what you can watch on television." The statement was an intentional distortion of fact by Rather and CBS. It was a perfect example of how the networks slant and twist their reporting.

When "60 Minutes" and Dan Rather were cleared in the slander suit brought by Dr. Carl Galloway, the California physician was disappointed but philosophical. He was quoted as saying, "It's not easy losing in public, but it's not a total loss; we raised some issues and made some points." And indeed, one critical point is worth noting. Though Rather and producer Steve Glauber were found not guilty of defamation of character, members of the jury did agree that the "60 Minutes" segment was "slanted."

## Distinction Blurred between Reporting News and Making News

The networks apparently are not above using entertainment programs to *make news*. In November 1982, a Catholic bishops' conference focused on the problem of priestly celibacy. Thousands of priests had left the church in order to marry. But television news focused on the bishops' disarmament statement. Priestly celibacy was not deemed newsworthy.

So why, on Palm Sunday, March 27, 1983, would the subject all of a sudden become news? Why would ABC at that time choose to focus attention on a subject which months before had been rejected? Sam Donaldson introduced the last story on "World News Tonight," March 27, with these words: "The church is now faced with a number of questions involving original principles versus changing times. Rebecca Chase examines one of the most troubling—the question of priestly celibacy." Chase quoted the National Opinion Research Center's prediction that "unless the celibacy law is changed by the year 2000, there will be a critical shortage of Catholic priests."

Now that sounds like news. But why was it news on March 27, 1983, when the issue was raised in November 1982? You may recall that March 27 also marked the premiere of *Thorn Birds,* the ABC miniseries about an Australian priest who breaks his vow of celibacy. *What an amazing coincidence.* And just two nights later, celibacy was news again in a special one-hour edition of "Nightline." Another amazing coincidence. For it was on that night in the ABC miniseries that the priest was shown committing adultery.

Surely something as valuable as the network news would not dare take its agenda from prime-time entertainment. And surely ABC's news division would never be used as a vehicle for generating interest for its entertainment programming. Because, if there is no clear-cut division between the news agenda and the entertainment agenda, then it follows that there can be no clear-cut distinction between entertainment and news, acting and journalism.

ABC News vice-president George Watson was quoted in *Channels* magazine. He made a remarkable statement concerning the *Thorn Birds*/ABC News connection. Watson said: "On an occasion when an entertainment event heightens interest in a particular topic, there is greater editorial justification to seize it when the interest is high." Watson went on to say: "The topic was out there. You're quite right in saying that we placed it out there. I see nothing wrong with that." That is an example of the fine art of *making* the news, not reporting it.

Without a doubt, television is the most powerful medium of influence—for good or evil—in our society. Do you remember when Ozzie and Harriet, Dick Van Dyke, Andy Griffith, and Mr. Ed played in prime-time television? It was in the early 1960s. Most would agree that the period from 1945 to 1965 was a morally conservative time—a good time to raise children. But with the student rebellion of the mid-60s, the moral base in America suffered rapid deterioration.

Traditional Christian values were assaulted in waves. First, there was the free-speech movement, which many called the "filthy" speech movement. Then followed the rock music movement, the recreational drug movement, and the free-sex movement.

According to Dr. James Hitchcock, in his book, *What Is Secular Humanism?* the youth rebellion could never have succeeded without important allies in the older generation—sympathetic professors, liberal clergy, permissive parents, and ambitious politicians.

But their number-one ally was the secular media. Media members welcomed, applauded, glorified, and promoted the attack on Christian values by the young rebels. Why? Because the young radicals' push for a wide-open, anything-goes society matched well the beliefs and biases of the leaders in the secular media.

It is extremely important to note that *the student activists were always a small minority.* But America viewed the movement through the lens of network television, and it *seemed* that the whole world was changing. The networks created that illusion for us.

When the "baby boomers" began to make anti-Christian noises on campus, the media took note. And that small minority was given the appearance of the majority by network television. Then dramatically, swiftly, the new morality, which is really the old immorality, began to take hold—aided and abetted by the national secular media.

## Liberal Media Has a Double Standard

American politics, especially the Washington, D.C. variety, always seem to give us the best examples of the media's double standard.

For example, it hasn't been long since the whole nation was appalled at the revelation of unethical and irresponsible sexual escapades of two of our congressmen on Capitol Hill. One involved a congressman's homosexual affair with a high school student, the other with a high school girl. There was no real negative outcry by the media. What outcry there was seemed to take the "kid gloves" approach. In a few days, even that had subsided, and the incidents were soon ignored if not forgotten.

After that, we witnessed the climax of a long and concerted effort to effect the resignation of presidential appointee James Watt from his post as Secretary of the Interior. Granted, Watt deserves no medal for tact. But, in the indignant cries from the media for his resignation, rarely if ever did we hear reference to his job performance. Watt's sharp tongue simply made him easy prey for his liberal opponents. And they won. James Watt resigned.

Now, to switch to still another scene. Many of the same media voices who spoke out boldly against Watt were strangely silent (even condoning) about the distasteful and disgusting performance by Joan Rivers on the Emmy Awards show. Rivers' barrage of blasphemy occurred only days before Watt's resignation.

She called Interior Secretary James Watt an "idiot," used God's name in vain, belittled her Jewish faith, and joked about herpes, prostitutes, and homosexuals. On top of that, she made her own crude cripple joke at the expense of the handicapped.

What was the response of the liberal national media? NBC stations all over the country received complaint calls from viewers. However, M.S. "Bud" Rykeyser, executive vice-president for public information for NBC, said he *was not aware of any complaints!* Rykeyser went on to say: "I thought it was a wonderful show and I thought Joan Rivers was a wonderful host." NBC News had reported heavily on the comments made by Watt leading up to Rivers' comments. However, NBC News ignored Rivers' comments. The double standard is visible even to the most unbiased viewer.

*Time* magazine sang Rivers' praises a few days later with a three-page feature, a totally positive piece of journalism. Emmy Awards coproducer Gary Smith called her the most important and funniest woman on television. Smith was quoted in one daily newspaper as saying Rivers "maintained an elegance and a dignity which set a tone for the entire show."

There is clearly a double standard in all of this. You can make your jokes and have your fun as long as your political and moral philosophy meets the approval of those who control the liberal national media. You can even do it on national prime-time television. And you will be praised for it.

But if your political or moral views differ from those of the national liberal media, expect the same treatment James Watt got.

The liberal secular media has influence and they use it. (In fact, when Lichter and Rothman asked the news elite who should have the most influence in running the country, they selected themselves!) Just one example of how they use this power is shown in the handling of the case of Dr. B. Samuel Hart.

On February 9, 1982, Sam Hart, a black evangelical broadcaster, was nominated by President Reagan to serve on the U.S. Civil Rights Commission. Even before the official announcement from the White House, attacks from the secular liberal media began pouring in. And they continued until three weeks later when Hart asked the President to withdraw his name from consideration. The media attacked Hart's evangelical position on moral issues. The following are some comments of the press concerning Hart. *Time* magazine: "An odd nominee for civil rights," a "rightwing religious nut," and "hostile to all the groups the commission is supposed to serve." The Philadelphia *Inquirer:* "A civil rights nominee offensive to human dignity." The Philadelphia *Daily News* called Hart a potential civil rights commissioner who didn't believe in civil rights. The publication went on to say that "Hart should leave the guardianship of civil rights to someone who believes all people have them." Then there was the *Washington Post* article stating that "Women's, civil rights, and gay groups called on President Reagan to withdraw the nomination of B. Sam Hart."

Dr. Hart said later that in listening to all the objections, he had learned that his nomination was being opposed primarily because he would be strongly pro-family. Eventually, the pressure of dealing with the media attack forced Hart to withdraw his nomination, thwarting President Reagan's attempt to put a recognized Christian in a place of influence.

Michael J. O'Neill, editor of the New York *Daily News*, stated concerning the media: "Have we become so arrogant with our power, so competitive that we cannot decide . . . that the First Amendment is often abused rather than served by those who would defend it?" O'Neill further stated that "there has been an astonishing growth in the power of the media in the last decade. I am by no means sure we are using it wisely. The extraordinary powers of the media, most convincingly displayed by network television and the national press, have been mobilized to influence major public issues and national elections, to help diffuse the authority of Congress and to disassemble the political parties—even to make presidents or break them. No longer do we merely cover the news. Thanks mainly to television, we are often partners now in the creation of news. . . . "

## Media Carefully Chooses Its Words

A well-chosen word—and what we have is, in reality, another form of subtle censorship. That's what the *Washington Post* must have in mind as it maintains its bias against conservative and traditional political attitudes. The *Post* is one of the nation's leading liberal media institutions. Another Washington newspaper recently reported that the *Post* uses the word "ultraconservative" with frequency, but the word "ultraliberal" does not appear to be in the *Post's* vocabulary.

A study conducted by the Committee for a Free Press revealed that the *Post* could bring itself to use "ultraliberal" only by putting it in quotes, giving it a fanatic slant and attributing it to those on the right. Using a computerized data retrieval system, the study showed that during the period surveyed, "ultraconservative" appeared forty-three times in the *Post's* news columns. "Ultraliberal" did not appear once except in quotes, "invariably attributed in a sarcastic manner to someone the *Post* considered to be ultraconservative." A similar pattern was found for the words "archconservative" and "archliberal."

The study also noted that the *Post* used the term "extreme right" for Margaret Thatcher's policies, the Heritage Foundation, and certain members of Congress. The *Post* called Senator Jesse Helms, the Virginia Republican Party, and the American Medical Association ultraconservative. The paper applied "far right" to Senator Helms, Margaret Thatcher's husband, and Latin American dictators.

Neither can individuals trust the networks to be accurate or factual when it comes to their historical docudramas, programs dealing with historical people or events presented as drama. They take the liberty to rewrite the history books and even change facts to their own liking.

The National Geographic Society criticized CBS for its distortion of historical fact in the CBS special, "Cook and Peary: The Race to the Pole." Robert Peary is credited with being the first man to reach the North Pole. His claim is well-documented and historically accepted. Dr. Frederick Cook claimed to have reached the Pole earlier, but had nothing to substantiate his claim.

The CBS production pictured Cook as reaching the North Pole first and left viewers with the impression that his legitimate claim was denied him by a vicious and paranoid Robert Peary. CBS even cast doubt on Peary's documented claim of reaching the Pole in 1909.

In its editorial, *National Geographic* pointed out that CBS failed to mention these historical facts concerning Cook. He attempted to publish an Indian dictionary—the work of another man—under his own name; he was discovered in a colossal fraudulent claim that he climbed Mount McKinley in Alaska; he served time in Leavenworth Penitentiary for mail fraud. (CBS implied that he was hounded into jail because of his North Pole claim.)

*National Geographic* said that CBS slandered an honest man and lifted up as hero a man whose life was characterized by grand frauds. The greatest fraud of all is that perpetrated against viewers who trust the networks.

Why do I no longer believe everything I hear reported or read? In the summer of 1982, my office was called by *People* magazine. The magazine told my secretary they wanted a comment from me concerning Morgan Fairchild, a star of the television program, "Flamingo Road." When told by my secretary of the call, I refused to return it because I felt that the magazine would distort any comment I gave. Much to my surprise, when the article came out there was a direct quote from me in the distorted fashion which I had suspected they would use if I had returned the call. When I called an editor about the quote and told him that I did not even talk with his magazine, he told me that the reporter had phoned my office, his reporter was experienced, and the magazine would stand by the quote!

You must also be aware that for some in the media, objective reporting has been replaced by advocacy reporting. If your views happen to coincide with the views of the one doing the reporting, the report will be favorable. If, however, your views differ from the one reporting, the report will be unfavorable. Gary Deeb, a syndicated columnist who writes for the Chicago *Sun-Times*, referred to me in one of his columns as a "rightwing religious zealot" despite the fact that Deeb knew practically nothing about my religious faith and had never once contacted me to discuss it.

Charles Colson, who began his very successful prison ministry following his conversion experience after being involved in Watergate, wrote a very important article which appeared in *Jubilee*, the newsletter of Prison Fellowship.

In the battle for the values our culture lives by, the weapons are often words. Take "gay" for example: a word connoting happiness is misused to mask perversion.

Or consider how abortionists are described as being for "free choice" (that's a good word), they are "progressive" (anything new is better), and are supported by "enlightened" interests. Anti-abortion groups, on the other hand, are against free choice, and therefore "regressive" and "bigoted."

Perhaps you've noticed how the Christian viewpoint is often labeled as "extreme fundamentalism" or coupled with inflammatory adjectives. The December 1981 court challenge to the Arkansas statute allowing Creationism to be taught as an alternative to evolution offers a vivid illustration. Consider how the *Washington Post* described the parties involved:

"The ACLU and the New York firm of Skadden Arps attacked the Arkansas law with a powerful case. Their brief is so good that there is talk of publishing it. Their witnesses gave brilliant little summaries of several fields of science, history, and religious philosophy." Such was the "enlightened" plaintiff.

The Creationist witnesses, however, were "impassioned believers, rebellious educators, and scientific oddities. All but one of the Creation scientists came from obscure colleges or Bible schools. The one who didn't said he believed diseases dropped from space, that evolution caused Nazism, and that insects may be more intelligent than humans but are hiding their abilities." It goes on.

The point is simple. If you were an uninformed reader, who would you believe—the firm of Skadden Arps with its brilliant summaries, or the backwoods weirdos from no-name colleges? One can only conclude that in Arkansas in December of 1981, to question evolutionary theory—that is, to be Christian—was to be stupid.

Editorial decisions can have far-reaching implications. One major American daily, for example, never uses the word "Christ" when speaking of Jesus. To do so, its editors believe, would be to make an editorial judgment.

Similarly, when Francis Schaeffer asked PBS to air his "How Shall We Then Live?", a presentation of history, Creation, and the universe from the Judeo-Christian perspective, he was turned down cold—"too religious."
But the same PBS regularly airs "Cosmos," feeding the viewer a steady diet of "The Cosmos is all that is or ever will be." That is as close to a definite catechism of humanism as one can find.

So the secular world gets prime-time coverage while the Christian world is exiled to its own programming. It's good to have our programs, of course—but by compartmentalizing us, the media effectively refuses to dignify the Christian view as a respectable intellectual alternative in the marketplace of ideas.

In all the voluminous coverage of Benigno Aquino's assassination, for example, I could find only one or two mentions of his Christian commitment.

But the fact is, it was Aquino's dramatic conversion to Christ which led him to return to the Philippines to "fight hatred with greater Christian love." By failing to see that spiritual truth, the media missed the story altogether.

So a word inserted here, a story ignored there, an interpretation and a nuance at a time, the secular view inexorably gains ground. And what astounds me is that we yell about the blatant eroticism and violence on television—as we should—yet virtually ignore the more insidious ways the media is seizing the mind of our culture.

"It is pretty clear from the entire pattern that the left-wing of American politics and culture has acquired a dictatorial veto power over the vocabulary of television. No word it objects to will survive in that medium." These were words spoken by Joe Sobran, a syndicated columnist, in an article titled "Networks Have the Last Word on Last Words." Sobran was simply confirming what Colson had written.

In the battle for the values our culture will live by, whether secular or Christian, much of the conflict involves words. Sobran's article mentions certain words which are taboo in television: "For instance, you won't hear an anchorman refer to the 'international Communist conspiracy.' Communism is an international movement, and its modus operandi is supremely underhanded. Month after month, KGB agents posing as diplomats and journalists are expelled from various free-world countries for stealing secrets, infiltrating peace movements, and for other assorted acts of mischief. The Soviets smuggle arms and money relentlessly to terrorists and guerillas." Yet, according to Sobran, certain strange "delicacies" prevail in the American media, "which will no more tolerate a reference to the 'international Communist conspiracy' than to the 'free world'—another taboo phrase."

Young people no longer engage in "promiscuous sex" or "immorality." Those words would be too judgmental. Instead, they are said to be "sexually active." Homosexuality is no longer a "perversion." "Gay" is a beautiful word not fraught with negative implications. "Adultery" has been supplanted by "affair." "Obscene" utterances are called "adult language." "Pornographic, smut" magazines are referred to as "sexually explicit materials."

Joe Sobran had a valid point. An increasingly liberal secular media has managed to transform the vocabulary of television. The change has been so complete that there remains practically no room for conservative maxims or words that bespeak Christian values.

Daniel Yankelovich, noted researcher on the media and founder and president of Yankelovich, Skelly, and White, Inc., had this to say about the media's use of the "freedom of the press" cry to cover their abuses and misuses of their power. "There is enormous importance attached to freedom of expression in this country. The press has nothing to worry about on that score. But, of course, they hide behind the First Amendment; they abuse the h— out of it."

## DISCUSSION AND REFLECTION QUESTIONS

1. Do you believe the national secular media is biased? In which direction?
2. Do you believe everything the media reports as they report it?
3. Have you ever noticed a news story attempting to shift public opinion by the use of suggestive words or phrases?
4. Do you think a Christian who actively practices his faith would be welcomed in the top layer of the national secular media? Why or why not?
5. Do you think the national secular media often tries to make news by providing massive favorable coverage to events or people they agree with? Why or why not?
6. Why does the media so often use terms like "ultraconservative" but rarely use terms such as "ultraliberal"?
7. Why are homosexuals now referred to as "gay" by the media rather than simply "homosexual" (or as "queer" as in past years)?

# TWELVE

# A CALL TO ACTION

Has our society already turned its back on the Christian view of man as the rule for law and justice, as the standard for determining right and wrong? I don't think that at this point in history we can truthfully answer that question. One thing, however, can be truthfully and honestly stated. If we have not already done so, we very soon will—unless there is an intentional, massive effort made by the Christian community to avoid it.

As I speak to various groups, I am appalled by the lack of knowledge or the level of concern regarding our moral and social situation. I simply find it hard to understand how anyone who takes his faith seriously can fail to see what *has happened* and what *is happening* in our society. Have we become so desensitized by the decay and corruption that we are dead to it all?

There are several kinds of reactions I get when I speak to those in the Christian community. First, there is the feeling that I have overstated the case and the situation isn't anywhere near as bad as I make it out to be. I hope these people are right. In fact, I pray to God that I am wrong. But having looked and lived with this concern day and night for seven years, I cannot honestly and intellectually say that I am overstating the problem.

Another reaction I get is best described by an incident that occurred among a small group of ministers to whom I spoke. After I had finished, one minister said: "I have no doubt that you are sincere, but in all I have heard you say you have been against something. I don't think Christians should be against. Christianity is not a religion of againstness." This attitude has probably done more than any other to encourage the moral situation which exists.

Such a mentality says that Christianity is for something, but not against anything. If one is to be for something, he must by necessity be against something. If one is for love, he is opposed to hate. If one is for salvation, he is opposed to sin. If one is for truth, he is opposed to falsehood. If one is for good, he is opposed to evil. I responded to the reply by saying that Jesus did not get crucified simply because He was for something. In fact, the straw which broke the camel's back and sealed His crucifixion was His turning over the tables of the moneychangers. He was against corruption in the temple. Jesus was against a lot of things: hate, sin, lust, lies, etc. To think that Christianity is only a religion for something is a false perception.

Another reaction I get is the usual flag-waving attitude about being against censorship. (In fact, immediately after the aforementioned minister said he didn't think Christians should be against something, a fellow minister also responded negatively toward me, saying that he was against censorship! He wasn't even aware that he had reinforced my previous point.) The people who raise the censorship issue usually haven't done any serious thinking concerning the situation and are only imitating what they have heard from the liberal secular media.

Legally, censorship is defined by the First Amendment: "Congress shall make no law . . . abridging the freedom of speech or of the press. . . . " Some people are naive enough to believe that the First Amendment means we can say anything, publish anything, or broadcast anything, anytime, anywhere. This is hardly the case.

## There Are Limitations

As Dr. Victor Cline of the University of Utah noted: "If we examine the First Amendment to our Constitution, we will note that there are many kinds of democratically enacted prohibitions of speech and expression. These, of course, can be amended or repealed any time we wish. Examples would include libel, slander, perjury, conspiracy, false advertising, excitement to violence, or speech that might create a 'clear and present danger,' such as yelling 'fire' in the crowded theater. Still other examples would include TV cigarette advertisements and also obscenity. In fact, most of the people who went to jail in the Watergate scandal did so because of what they said—or for words they spoke (e.g., perjury and conspiracy)."

I asked my fellow minister if he would be willing for information on building an atomic bomb to be published so that anyone with a seventh-grade education could build one? Then I asked him if he wanted the local drugstore to sell pornographic magazines featuring children? He was opposed to both. So he wasn't really against censorship.

Censorship has existed since man learned to communicate. It is part of life. When the networks decide what programs to show and what programs not to show, that is censorship. They have imposed their standards, their tastes, their values, and their morals on the public. They have denied the public the privilege of seeing a program which they have refused to air.

When editors decide what to put in their newspaper, or what to leave out, they are practicing censorship. Ask them if they believe in censorship, and they would say no. Yet they practice that in which they say they don't believe. Now the editors would call their practice editing, but it is nothing except another form of censorship. A rose by another name, the poet said, would still be a rose.

When librarians decide which books to place in the library, they are practicing censorship. When radio and TV newscasters decide what to report and what to ignore, they are practicing censorship. When book editors decide what material to include in school textbooks and what material to leave out, or even how to present that which they do, they are practicing censorship.

Censorship exists in our society. In fact, it cannot keep from existing as long as man continues to communicate. The irony of it all is that those who are the quickest to cry "censorship" are often the ones who practice censorship the most.

Other well-meaning people tell me they don't believe in boycotts. I doubt very seriously that if these people took their car to a shop where they were cursed, their children abused, the work was shoddy, and they were grossly overcharged, that they would have the slightest reservations about boycotting that shop in the future. Again, this mentality is the result of listening too much to the secular liberal media and doing too little serious thinking for oneself.

Brought into all of this is the responsibility of Christian stewardship. What we have is not ours. It belongs to God. We are His stewards. He has entrusted creation to us to use to His glory. Supporting companies which exploit people and deny the Christian concept of man simply isn't good Christian stewardship.

Have we already passed the point of no return? We very well may have. My opinion is that if the church isn't able to slowly turn the tide of filth promoted by the humanist philosophy within the next few years (five at most), then the battle is over and we will indeed be living in the post-Christian era. It is that critical.

Why do ˌ say this? Because this humanist philosophy has become so engrained in our society, so accepted even by multitudes within the church, that in another five years it will become set like concrete.

## What Should the Church Do?
What should the church do to regain its position and prevent the post-Christian era? Answering that question isn't easy, and I don't claim to have all the answers. I do, however, offer these suggestions.

The church must immediately begin a massive education program. Our people simply are not aware of the magnitude or seriousness of the situation and therefore cannot effectively come to grips with it. This educational process must involve the Sunday School program, the worship services, and the other educational arms of the church.

The various denominations need to call together their top leaders to educate them concerning the problem and plan a course of action for their own denomination. It is imperative, however, that the various denominations cooperate in addressing the problem. We simply can no longer afford the luxury of "doing our own thing." We must forget our minor theological differences for the sake of the whole church and its future.

The church must ask for and secure the strong enforcement of existing laws regarding pornography and, where needed, secure passage of new laws to deal with the situation. We must train our people in the process of selective buying. We must arouse the public to the situation. We must make our political leaders aware of our stand and expect and demand more response from them. Individual Christians must become involved in the political process as an expression of their Christian faith. We must see through the false application of the cry "separation of church and state." It has come to mean that the state cannot be influenced by Christianity. That is a false interpretation and application.

We must let companies which provide money to make possible pornographic magazines and materials know that they will no longer receive the financial support of the Christian community. The same must be done with companies which help promote violent, vulgar, profane, and anti-Christian television programs.

## What You Can Do
You can seek involvement by your church and your denomination. My friend Bill Kelly, a retired FBI agent, tells of an instance in

which prospective jurors were asked three questions. "Have you, or anyone in your family, been a victim of sexual abuse?" About 10 percent of the prospective jurors raised their hands. "Have you ever read or even paged through a pornographic magazine?" About 40 percent replied they had. Finally, this question. "Have you ever heard a sermon on pornography or obscenity?" Not a single hand was raised. What a powerful indictment of the clergy!

Approach your minister in a loving and kind way, present the facts, and ask that he preach on the subject or lead the congregation in a study on the subject. Ask that your church get involved.

Next, write the very top officials in your denomination and request that they make the war against obscenity, pornography, and indecency a top priority item within your denomination.

You can also pray. Pray for those responsible for pornography, that God would touch their hearts and change their minds. We must learn to hate the sin and still be able to love the sinner. Pray for the victims of pornography and the assault on Christian values by the media. Pray for those who are fighting the battle on the front lines. Pray that the body of Christ, the church, will become involved before it is too late.

You can become informed. Read the newspapers to become more aware of the negative consequences of violent and vulgar programs, pornography, or indecency. Study the movie ads to see the types of movies showing in your community. From time to time, watch programs or movies which offend you so that you can be aware of the seriousness of the problem. Subscribe to publications which will help keep you informed.

Study the laws of your state and community. Seek enforcement of existing laws and enactment of laws which are needed. Seek out public officials and find their attitude toward the problem. Become involved in politics. Register and vote. Work in behalf of candidates committed to the Christian view of man. Contribute to their campaigns.

You can speak out. Let the stores where you shop know you will not continue doing business with them as long as they continue to sell pornography. Let the television sponsors know you will no longer buy their products as long as they continue to sponsor anti-Christian, violent, vulgar, and profane programs. Join organized boycotts. Encourage others to join boycotts. Get your church to urge members to join boycotts. Boycotting for Christians is simply part of their Christian stewardship.

Write to your elected officials. Write to companies which help sponsor degrading television programs. Write to companies which sell or advertise in pornographic publications.

Help organize a citizens' group in your community. Work as a team.

Inform others. Share materials with them so they too can become informed and motivated. Use your phone to let your voice be heard. Write letters to the editor of your local and denominational papers. Use talk shows to express your opinions.

Join national organizations working to correct the problem. A small annual donation will bring you the informative material provided regularly from any of these organizations·

National Federation for Decency
P.O. Box 2440
Tupelo, Mississippi 38803

This is the organization I head. We will provide information on the problem on a general basis. Our *NFD Journal,* published ten times a year, is available for only $15 annually.

Morality in Media, Inc.
475 Riverside Drive
New York, New York 10115

This organization, headed by my good friend Father Morton Hill, specializes in fighting cable porn. Legal resources are available.

Citizens for Decency through Law
2331 West Royal Palm Road #105
Phoenix, Arizona 85021

This organization deals with the legal aspects of pornography. Legal assistance is available.

Why is it necessary to look at samples of pornography, attend certain movies, or watch certain offensive television programs? My good friend Paul Tanner, executive secretary of the Church of God (Anderson, Indiana) has written the following concerning this:

Because all too many people do not know what the pornographers are peddling. Often legislators and law enforcement officials do not even know . . . let alone preachers and Christians who have been protected from the world.

I know I am vulnerable. I know any adult who inspects this scum is vulnerable. If there is any doubt whatsoever about your motives—don't! But it wasn't until I saw some pictures of child and *infant* abuse that the fire began to burn in my bones. Until we really know, we won't get angry enough to fight.

I hate it. It makes me sick, but I liken it to a physician inspecting cancer. You have a choice. You can inspect it now, or wait until your children do. They can't help it. It's everywhere. It circulates around the junior high schools.

The pornographers don't want you to inspect it. They want to continue to exploit our ignorance and steal the money and minds of men.

This filth does not reflect the will of the people, but the will of the pornographers.

If you are going to talk about it, you must know about it. You must see for yourself. And you must hate it as God hates it, like a physician hates cancer.

I suggest that when becoming acquainted with this material, it always be done with another adult who knows and shares fully your purpose for becoming informed.

## Long-range Actions Needed

All of these things, of course, are only immediate, short-range actions which we must take. Other actions will take more time. Our denominations must enlarge their narrow-minded tunnel vision of "social" concerns from only those which are civil to also include those which are moral. Our view of the Gospel has been too narrow, especially in the larger denominations.

We must, in our churches, do a better job teaching and preaching the fundamentals of the faith. Certainly we cannot stop with the fundamentals, but neither can we ignore them as we have for the past several decades. In many of our churches, people are biblically illiterate.

There must be a deeper awareness of and a recommitment to our faith. In the course of it all, lines will have to be drawn. We have tried to be inclusive in our faith (and we should have); now we will have to be exclusive. Not every idea or philosophy which comes along is compatible with the Christian view of man. We must reassert our faith in the marketplace and in daily living. We must act on the Christian view of man in our political system. This will need to be done not in an arrogant or offensive manner, but with love and meekness. We must not, however, confuse love and meekness with weakness.

We have taken our faith and our heritage too lightly, as if it would continue indefinitely regardless of what we do or fail to do. We must remember that our society, based on the Christian view of man, is still an experiment—not a finished product. It can be lost, changed to one where man becomes God. The results of that change would be awesome. Human life would be only convenience and individual freedoms discarded for "the good of society." If the church fails now, our failure will adversely affect generations to come. I seriously doubt, if we fail now, that there will ever again be a society based on the Christian view of man in our country. If there is one, it will be centuries before it begins. The suffering, persecution, and pain caused by the failure of the church to successfully address this situation will be immeasurable.

Earlier I stated five steps of regression in ridding our society of Christian influence: (1) ignore the church and censor it as an integral part of our society; (2) question the church and present one-sided arguments belittling it; (3) attack the church verbally; (4) ostracize from the mainstream of society those who would overtly practice their faith; and (5) physically persecute those who would practice their Christian faith.

We are now in step four. The decision as to whether step five comes is, at this point, still in the hands of the Christian community. Without dedicated, concentrated effort now, in another five years the decision will no longer be ours to make. Isn't a society based on the Christian view of man worth our best efforts to preserve?

## DISCUSSION AND REFLECTION QUESTIONS

1. Do you agree with the author that the very foundation of Western civilization, the Christian view of man as a basis for government, is under serious attack?
2. Do you feel the problem is as bad as the author thinks it is?
3. In order to be for something, is it also necessary at times to be against something?
4. Does the First Amendment give everyone the right to print or

broadcast anything he desires, whenever he desires?

5. When the networks depict Christians in a biased manner and refuse to allow positive portrayals of Christians in a modern-day setting, is that censorship?

6. Does Christian stewardship involve careful selection of the products we buy, i.e., refusal to buy from companies which help support pornography or anti-Christian television programs?

7. Should the church be addressing the immorality and biases of the media?

8. Is the foundation of our government indestructible?

9. Could it be possible, in our society, that Christians would be physically persecuted for practicing their faith?

# CLICHÉ ARGUMENTS

Those who get involved in the battle for decency will sooner or later run into some or all of the following cliché arguments. We hope that the answers will prove helpful in your fight for decency.

**What right do you have to tell me what I can watch on television?**
The question is faulty. Only the networks and local stations decide what is going to be on television. The proper question is, *"What right do you have to become involved in the process of deciding what is to be shown on television?"* And we have every right. Each local station is licensed by the government to broadcast in the public interest. The Federal Communications Commission encourages the public to become involved in the broadcasting process. Even the National Association of Broadcasters, in its code of ethics, encourages individuals and parents to become involved and make their views known to the broadcasting industry. We have been told to become involved in the process by our government and by the broadcasting industry itself. Would you deny us that right?

**Some people like to see violence and sex and hear profanity on television. Shouldn't they have the right?**
Some people would like to see child pornography on television. Shouldn't they have that right? That some people would like to see something on television is no reason for any program to be on television. All programs should add to and make a positive contribution to man's cultural, social, mental, emotional, and spiritual heritage in an informative and entertaining manner and not appeal to nor exploit man's prurient nature.

**Do you believe in censorship?**
When asked this question, simply throw it back to the one who asked it. "Do you believe in censorship?" (The usual answer is, "No, I do not.") Follow up by asking, "Do you believe it is OK to

show child pornography on television?" Unless totally devoid of morals, taste, and common sense, this person has climbed into his own trap.

Ever since communication began, there has been censorship. Every word ever printed, every word or scene ever aired has been censored. It all depends on who is doing the censoring. Are we for government censorship of usual programming? No. We are for corporate responsibility on the part of the networks as well as by the sponsors.


**If you don't like what is on, turn off the television. That will solve the problem.**
Would you also say to me if you don't like crime in the streets, stay in your house? Would you say to me if you don't like drunk drivers, stay off the highways? We live in a society, not as a group of isolated individuals. To illustrate this: A mother and her young daughter in California watched an exceptionally good movie on television entitled *Born Free.* When the same network (NBC) carried a movie entitled *Born Innocent,* the mother and daughter thought it might be the same type of movie and began to watch. Very early in the program was a graphic scene of a young girl being raped with a plumber's helper. The mother immediately got up and turned off the set. The mother said that scenes such as that should not be permitted, that some child might be negatively impressed and commit the same act. Two days later, her nine-year-old daughter was raped with a beer bottle by a gang of children and youth. The children and youth were imitating the movie they had seen on television. Turning off the television is noninvolvement and problems are never solved that way.


**Do you presume you have the right to tell an advertiser which programs he can help sponsor?**
We don't tell an advertiser which programs he can help sponsor. The advertiser makes that decision. We cannot tell him where to spend his money because it is his money to spend. But we have an equal right to spend our money where we desire just as that advertiser does. And if the advertiser wants to put his money into low-quality, immoral, or anti-Christian programming, then we certainly have the right to spend our money with other advertisers and to encourage our friends to do the same. In fact, we have a responsibility to spend our money where it will do the most good.

**Aren't there other things wrong with our society with which you could better spend your time than television?**
Certainly there is an abundance of things wrong with our society other than television. However, we are concerned with television because it has the potential to be the most constructive medium in the history of mankind. Instead of developing that potential, television seems headed in the opposite direction. Indeed, if television has the potential to be the most constructive medium in the history of mankind, it also has the potential for being the most destructive medium. We are involved because we desire television to reach its constructive potential, not its destructive potential. We care deeply about our society, about our families, about our neighbors. We want the best possible environment in which to live, work, and raise our children.

**Don't you think television should deal frankly with reality? After all, violence, sex, and profanity—and rejecting those values which spring from the Judeo-Christian ethic—is a part of the world in which we live.**
Yes, television should deal with the real world. But love, truth, compassion, beauty, and other positive values are also a part of the real world. Why should television dwell primarily on the ugly and ignore that which is beautiful?

**Watching television has never corrupted anyone; neither has a book ever corrupted anyone.**
Then watching television has never helped anyone and reading a book has never helped anyone. If that be true, we should do away with all our schools because they aren't doing any good. No, the truth of the matter is that good programs project good images and poor programs project poor images. We should remember that all television is educational television and ask ourselves what television is teaching. Currently, it is teaching that sex has no morals attached, that violence is a legitimate way to solve conflict, and that profanity is acceptable language. Television too often ridicules those values which made our country strong and which we have long held as worthwhile to pursue. This can only have a detrimental effect on our society.

The following arguments and answers are supplied by Morality in Media, an organization which deals primarily with pornography, and is headed by my friend Father Morton Hill.

**Pornography is harmless. A Presidential Commission report said so.**
(1) The Majority Report of the Presidential Commission on Obscenity and Pornography was called a "scientific scandal" by many in the scientific community. It was rejected by the U.S. Senate by a vote of sixty to five. The Hill-Link Minority Report of that Commission was read into the record in both houses of Congress as a "responsible position on the issues." The Hill-Link Report cited numerous instances where evidence was suppressed when it went counter to the predetermined "findings" of the majority report. The Hill-Link Report and the chapters by Dr. Victor B. Cline in *Where Do You Draw the Line?* exposed the majority report for what it was. In addition, studies in the Hill-Link Report show linkages between exposure to obscene material and sexual deviancy, promiscuity, affiliation with criminal groups, and more. However, extremists who want obscenity laws repealed (as the majority report recommended) began a campaign in early 1977 to have the report resurrected and considered a reportable document.

(2) The Supreme Court in *Paris Theatre v. Slaton* (June, 1973) said: "The sum of experience, including that of the past two decades, affords an ample basis for legislatures to conclude that a sensitive, key relationship of human existence, central to family life, community welfare, and the development of human personality, can be debased and distorted by crass commercial exploitation of sex."

**You can't legislate morality.**
On its face, this cliché is absurd because every law legislates morality. Every law sets some standard for its citizens and every citizen must ultimately make the moral decision to obey or disobey.

Private morals are private; public morals are the business of the entire community; and the officers empowered by the community are to defend the welfare of the community against the willful minority. Commercial obscenity is public business. It is public morality that obscenity laws are designed to safeguard, not private morality.

**Obscenity is in the eye of the beholder. What is obscene to you may not be obscene to others.**
This implies that obscenity is subjective. It is not. It is the description or depiction of specific sexual activity, the description or depiction of which is prohibited by law, to protect the common good. It is as objective as stealing or murder.

**I'd rather see people make love than violence.**

There is no love in pornography. It is totally loveless, debasing women, children, and humanity in general. In addition, violence is inherent in pornography.

**War, poverty, hunger, and violence are the real obscenities. Sex is not obscene.**
The extension of the word "obscenity" to cover all kinds of social evils is a recent development in our language. It is a well-known technique to confuse and blunt the force of obscenity law.

Of course, sex is not obscene. It is the design and creation of God. It is the debasing abuse of sex that is obscene. And as in the past, so now all over the country, legislatures and the judiciary definitely specify certain abuses of sex as obscene.

**If you don't like pornographic films and books, you don't have to see them or buy them, but don't interfere with my right to see or buy them.**
I don't see or buy pornography. But it is there polluting the environment in which I am trying to raise my children. Society says it does not want it there and has enacted laws against it.

The United States Supreme Court has said that what you do in the privacy of your home is your own business. But your privacy right does not extend to the marketplace. It is against the law for anyone to sell or exhibit obscenity to you.

**Freedom of expression is protected by the First Amendment.**
It most certainly is. But the Supreme Court has said and always held that obscenity is not protected by the First Amendment. It is not protected expression, any more than libel or slander are. Obscenity is not a First Amendment issue. It is a crime, and most of the traffic in hard core pornography in the country is controlled by organized crime.

**Who are you to tell me what I can see or read? You are imposing your morality on me.**
Nobody can tell you what to see or to read. But the community can tell you what commercial spectacles and literature cannot be sold or distributed to you—if you choose to live in that community. The community sets up standards for itself and has a right to legislate to protect those standards.

Nobody is imposing his morality on anybody. It is only the consensus of the community that determines the standards of public decency. When that consensus is properly manifested in public law, that is community or public morality, not "ours."

**Obscenity is a victimless crime.**
There is no such thing as a "victimless crime." In every crime there is a seller or seducer, and the person who purchases or the seduced. That person is the immediate victim, and society is the ultimate victim, for with each seduction the moral fabric of society is diminished. The "victimless crimes" theory is an active and *insidious* attack on almost all laws dealing with public morality, maintaining there is "no victim" when "consenting adults" indulge in drugs, prostitution, obscenity, homosexuality, adultery, incest, gambling, etc.

A glaring instance of victimization in obscenity are the children used in child pornography.

For centuries, civil communities have maintained laws against such behavior as detrimental to the public health, morals and welfare.

**When "consenting adults" go to see a dirty movie, no one is being harmed.**
Regarding so-called "consenting adults," the United States Supreme Court said in *Paris Theatre* (June, 1973): "We categorically disapprove the theory that obscene films acquire constitutional immunity from state regulation simply because they are exhibited for consenting adults only. Rights and interests other than those of the advocates are involved. These include the interest of the public in the quality of life, the total community environment, the tone of commerce and, possibly, the public safety itself." (If we followed the "consenting adults" theory, we would have never outlawed dueling in this country.)

**If pornography were allowed to flow freely people would get bored and the problem would take care of itself.**
This boredom or satiation theory is invalid. (See *Where Do You Draw the Line?* edited by Dr. Victor B. Cline.) Heavy users of pornography do not get bored. They go deeper and deeper into more and more bizarre forms of it. Pornography is addicting.

Denmark is often brought up when the boredom theory is espoused. Denmark legalized pornography, the argument goes, and porn profits dropped because people got bored.

Denmark's porn profits are falling, but not because of boredom.

189

Underworld infiltration of the porn industry, gangland violence, and tie-ins with traffic in narcotics forced Copenhagen police to close down dozens of smut dens, and all live sex shows have been outlawed (Associated Press reports, 1972-1976).

Remember, every day children are seeing pornography for the first time. Pornography strikes at children in the mails, on newsstands, etc.

**How do you define obscenity?**
How I define obscenity is not the issue. The Supreme Court has defined obscenity to the satisfaction of most. It said obscene materials are those which "taken as a whole appeal to the prurient interest in sex, which portray sexual conduct in a patently offensive way, and which, taken as a whole, do not have serious literary, artistic, political, or scientific value."

**But the Supreme Court left it to communities to decide what is obscene.**
This is an oversimplification and a misleading one. Community standards is not *the* test for obscenity, but a *part* of the test for obscenity, and has been part of the test for obscenity since 1957. In 1973, the Court said: "The basic guidelines for the trier of the fact must be: (a) whether 'the average person, applying contemporary community standards' would find that the work, taken as a whole appeals to the prurient interest . . . (b) whether the work depicts or describes, in a patently offensive way, sexual conduct specifically defined by the applicable state law," etc. It is the "trier of the fact," a jury or a judge who decides what is obscene under the guidelines.

**How is a producer or publisher to know his material is obscene when the Supreme Court can't even decide what is obscene?**
The court has decided what is obscene. It is up to a person who traffics in pornography to be alert to and know what the Supreme Court decisions are. The Court said in its landmark *Miller* decision when it defined obscenity, "We are satisfied that these prerequisites (the three-part test) will provide fair notice to a dealer in such materials that his public and commercial activities may bring prosecution."

**Why be concerned about obscenity when there is so much violent crime?**

190

They're related. Pornography outlets breed and attract violent crime.

The porno industry is flourishing and growing, so the American people must want it or simply don't care.
Certainly there are some who want it. That's what makes it so profitable. And obviously there are some who don't care. But all surveys show that the majority of Americans are vehemently opposed to the traffic in pornography and want it stopped. The majority do care, but they are confused and discouraged in the face of a highly organized industry and the loud prophets of false freedom.
One of the major factors in the growth of the pornography traffic is the lack of vigorous enforcement of obscenity laws, particularly at the federal level.
If we are to follow this argument, then absolutely nothing will be illegal because there is a certain demand for all things.

Why bother enforcing the law? The adult bookstores and porno movie houses keep operating while their owners are in the courts.
Continuous, vigorous enforcement of the law is the answer. When arrests and prosecutions begin, the sex industry is put on warning. Prison sentences, fines, and legal fees will put the pornographers out of business. Atlanta, Jacksonville, and Cincinnati have rid their cities of a great deal of pornography through vigorous, continuous enforcement of the law. And experts say that with aggressive enforcement of federal law, the back of the porno industry would be broken in eighteen months.

But I want to see porno programming in my home and I pay to see it.
You might pay for it, but once the cable operator transmits pornography through that wire, it is released to the community. It becomes the community's business, and the community can legislate against it. And the law is aimed, not at you, but at the cable operator who transmits the cableporn to you. You might also want heroin in your home and pay for it, but it is against the law for the seller to sell it to you.

The cable operator says only those who pay for cableporn will get it, so if you don't want it, you don't have to subscribe to it.
Again, once the cableporn is released to the community, it is the community's business. In addition, there have been complaints from

191

many areas of the country that the signals of cableporn channels are "bleeding" over onto the sets of people who don't subscribe to them. Audio signals are clear and unscrambled; video signals fade in and out clearly.

There is no lock box that is a match for a child's curiosity. Children in Michigan have already found a way to bring a cableporn channel into nonsubscribing homes simply by jiggling the key on the cable channel selector. In addition, it came out in a Utah case that one key opens every lock box.

**In trying to get a law passed that prohibits cableporn, you're trying to tell me what I can see.**
Nobody can tell you what you can see. But the community can tell you what cannot be transmitted through the cable wires if it chooses to do so. The community sets up standards for itself and has a right to legislate to protect those standards.

**A law prohibiting cableporn would interfere with the First Amendment rights of the cable operator, with the free flow of information.**
There is already a federal law prohibiting the broadcasting of the obscene, indecent, and profane, and it has never interfered with the free flow of information in broadcasting. Cable casting, the U.S. Department of Justice has decided, does not come under the purview of the broadcasting law because it is transmitted through wires. There is almost no regulation on cable TV and there should be. There should be the same regulation of cable as there is of broadcasting. Different technology or not, it comes through the same instrument, the TV set, into the home.

**If you don't want cableporn bleeding over onto your set, don't subscribe to cable at all.**
Nobody should have to deprive himself of cable TV because a few porno peddlers are giving the industry a bad name. Cable TV is a medium of magnificent potential, of infinite variety.